THE MAHOGANY MAFIA

Also By
ADAM ROUSSELLE SR.

ROUX'S WAR

Profile Of An American Soldier

COUNTING CROWNS

Catching Timber Thieves From Space

U|R|M|C

Revolutionizing The Energy Industry

SHORT CIRCUIT

Uncovering America's Largest Fraud

THE BASTARDS ARE BACK

Uncle Warren's 1951 Warning From Korea On Russian and Chinese Infiltration and Today's Battle For America's Homeland Security

THE MAHOGANY MAFIA

By:

ADAM ROUSSELLE SR.

Adam Rousselle Sr.

Self-Published

2113 Middle Street

Sullivans Island, South Carolina 29482

Copyright © 2024 by Adam Rousselle Sr.

All Rights Reserved. This book, or any parts thereof, may not be

Reproduced in any form without permission.

Published simultaneously in Canada and The United Kingdom

Library Of Congress Cataloging-In-Publications Data

Rousselle, Adam 2024.

The Mahogany Mafia: Murder and Conspiracy In The Jungle

ISBN: 979-8-9920617-5-8

Series: Alacrity and Dispatch: Chronicles of a Citizen-Soldier's Selfless Service, Book Two

Genre: Autobiography & Biography/ Memoir; True Crime; Action & Adventure.

BISG Number (Book Industry Study Group)

TRU003000 TRUE CRIME / Organized Crime

BIO023000 BIOGRAPHY & AUTOBIOGRAPHY / Adventurers & Explorers

BIO026000 BIOGRAPHY & AUTOBIOGRAPHY / Memoirs

Library Of Congress Control Number (LCCN): 2024925763

United States Copyright Office Registration Number: TXu 2-454-374 August 31, 2024

Printed in the United State Of America

This book is printed on acid free paper

Book design by Adam Rousselle Sr.

THIS BOOK IS DEDICATED TO:

<u>My family</u>:
My indefatigable mother, Joyce
Catherine, Adam, Hayden, and Benjamin—
I hope this book helps you understand our lives better.

<u>My Brothers and Sister</u>:

Joey, Jim, Joe Jr., Dave, Rick, Billy, Kevin, Daniel, Josh, Brian and Effervescent Eve.

<u>My Mentors</u>:

Les Thatcher; Jeff Bracker; Lyle Sussman; Dean Robert Taylor; Susan Boardman Russ; Clint Vince and Steve Weber

<u>Special Recognition to those whose work directly impacted this story:</u>

Michael 'Blue 1 Tango' Reiber

Lindi J. Quackenbush

Tuomo Kauranne

Vesa Leppanen

Hon. Senator Mitch McConnell

Billy Piper: Thank you for listening and acting

In Memory of:

Emily Claire Leonard

Foreign Service Officer

Her courage and lifelong activities to support voiceless Americans in harm's way inspires me, still.

Hon. Michael Fitzpatrick

With unparalleled courage, he personally confronted a Honduran prison warden, demanding the release of his constituents. His boldness and unwavering commitment to justice remain an enduring testament to his character.

Why I Write: *The Promise of America*

I write because I believe in the promise of America—not just as a nation, but as an idea: that no matter how hard the road, no matter how impossible the odds, we can build a better world through courage, sacrifice, and an unrelenting will to serve others.

My experiences are proof of that promise. From the battlefields where I learned the true meaning of selfless service, to the jungles where I fought to reclaim justice for my family, to the courtroom and beyond—I've dedicated my life to standing up for those who can't stand for themselves.

Even if you don't know it, I've fought for you—and for a generous America that lifts up those who embody quiet courage, resilience, and hope; souls who fight their own battles every day—in small towns across this great nation—living the very promise our ancestors knew we could achieve.

Through the Alacrity and Dispatch series, I share stories of resilience, ingenuity, and hope. These books aren't just accounts of what I've done—they're testaments to the belief that one person, armed with truth and purpose, can gather teams of like-minds toward a common good and deliver extraordinary change. They remind us that the American Dream isn't just something you chase; it's something you fight for, no matter the cost.

I write to inspire you—to prove that no obstacle is insurmountable, no injustice unshakable, and no dream beyond reach. I write to remind you that American patriotism isn't about words—it's about action. It's about showing up, standing firm, and never giving up, even when the fight seems endless.

As you fight your own battles and chase your American dream, I offer a spirit—both American and human—that endures and overcomes. This is my way of delivering indefatigable hope that the best is yet to come for you and our Nation.

Prologue

Since 1760, the Mosquito Coast within the Olancho region of Honduras has been a key source of prized Honduran Mahogany.

In 1864 Colonels Barahona, Zavala, and Antúnez from Olancho started The Olancho War against the Honduran government fighting against slave labor in the timber trade, land rights, representation, and cultural preservation.

1,200 died in that war. Additionally, 500 were then executed by hanging, 200 were shot, and 600 families were exiled from Olancho.

Since 1924 an average of 27 tractor-trailer loads of Mahogany have been harvested from Olancho. That's 27, every single day, for 100 years.

A 70-year-old sign remains along the only highway into Olanchito. Translated it reads: "Enter if You Like, Leave if You Can."

I first entered Honduras as a U.S. soldier with the 7th Special Forces Group (Airborne) tasked with training the Contras in the Honduran Jungle. After being Honorably Discharged from the Army following the Iraqi Invasion, I decided to return to Honduras to build a sawmill and launch a lumber business.

We became the 3rd largest business in Honduras.

Today, I can never return to the country.

Murder, conspiracy, theft, and intrigue, orchestrated by the deepest levels of corruption in the Honduran government; I saw it all. This is my story.

Chapter 1.	The Return Of Gringo Joe	1
Chapter 2.	Hyper-Vigilance and IRC 936	4
Chapter 3.	All Or Nothing	10
Chapter 4.	The Return Of Gringo Joe	21
Chapter 5.	The Best No Chicken Money	30
Chapter 6.	Be Careful What You Ask For	43
Chapter 7.	Corruption And Betrayal	50
Chapter 8.	Resolute Decisions	64
Chapter 9.	Bracing For Impact	69
Chapter 10.	Frogs In Boiling Water	75
Chapter 11.	Gold Shotguns, And A Proposal	82
Chapter 12.	Every Decision Has A Price	90
Chapter 13.	Reflections In Paris	96
Chapter 14.	Treachery	102
Chapter 15.	Turning Point	109
Chapter 16.	Honduras Is Burning	118
Chapter 17.	A New Direction	132
Chapter 18.	And Then There Were Three	139
Chapter 19.	One Last Phone Call	154
A Glimpse Ahead		162

Chapter 1.   The Return Of Gringo Joe

The jungle felt familiar but unforgiving. As I stood beneath the sprawling canopy, I couldn't help but reflect on the journey that had brought me here. War had shaped me, honed my instincts, and taught me to survive under the most harrowing conditions. But nothing in my military training had prepared me for what awaited in the Honduran jungle—the web of corruption, greed, and violence orchestrated by The Mahogany Mafia.

I had thought the scars of war were the heaviest burden I'd ever carry, but I was wrong. Here, survival wasn't just about endurance; it was about navigating a shadowy world where every ally could be a traitor, and every decision could cost lives.

Later that morning, I stood on the balcony of my modest office, staring out over the dense, vibrant jungle that stretched as far as the eye could see. The sun was beginning its descent, casting a golden hue over the landscape. But I had no time to admire the beauty around me. My mind was consumed by the urgent crisis unfolding in my timber business.

A sharp knock on the door broke my concentration. I turned to see my trusted general manager, Jimmy Malone, entering the room, twisting his moustache with a worried expression.

"Adam, we just received word from Olanchito, another shipment has been hijacked. The locals are getting really angry, and our clients are threatening to pull out if we can't secure the deliveries."

I ran a hand through my hair, feeling the weight of the situation pressing down on me. I knew that the stakes were high. This was not just about business; it was about survival in a land where corruption and danger lurked around every corner.

"We need to figure this out Jimmy. Double the security detail and try to negotiate with the local leaders. We can't afford any more losses and neither can they. We are on the same team with them, remind them of that and tell them I am coming to meet with Sr. Maquez, in Olanchito, in person, on Monday" I said, my voice steady but tinged with frustration.

As Jimmy left to find a landline to make the call and execute the plan, my thoughts drifted back to my father, Joe Rousselle, or "Gringo Joe" as he was known in Honduras. Dad had always been a larger-than-life figure, full of charm and audacity. His entrepreneurial spirit had led him to Honduras years ago, where he carved out a niche for himself in the most unexpected of ways.

I remembered the first time I reconnected with my father after joining the Army. Dad was living in a small coastal town, surrounded by people who admired his charisma and business acumen. Joe's life was a stark contrast to the disciplined, structured world I had grown accustomed to in the military.

He lived above the Pharmacia Nueva with Argentina de Batres. Their house was modest but exuded an air of comfort and affluence. I found myself drawn to the stories my father told about his life in Honduras. Gringo Joe had made a name for himself by importing and selling personal hygiene products, a venture that seemed trivial but was surprisingly lucrative in the local market.

"Adam, you've got to understand something," he said one evening over dinner. "Opportunities are everywhere if you know where to look. You've just got to attack them at the right moment."

His words were nearly the same as we used in combat, perhaps he intended so. His words served as a guiding principle in my own entrepreneurial journey. Despite the complexities of our relationship, I couldn't deny the impact my father had on shaping my worldview.

I snapped back to the present as my phone rang loudly on the desk, few folks had this warehouse number, and it was likely from overseas. My heart skipped a beat as I answered.

"Mr. Rousselle, This is the Palmerola Airforce Base operator, hold for a patch from Joseph Rousselle" Adam, it's Dad." Gringo Joe's voice came through the line, as confident and commanding as ever. "I'm back in Honduras. We need to talk." It had the unmistakable tone that someone else was listening.

The timing couldn't have been worse. My business was teetering on the edge, and the return of my father, with all his schemes and ambitions, could either be a lifeline or a disaster.

"Dad, I'm dealing with a lot right now. Jimmy's up here. Can this wait?" I tried to keep my tone neutral.

"No, it can't. I have a idea that could turn things around. Meet me in La Ceiba tomorrow evening." The line went dead.

Dad had a way of pulling me into his whirlwind of plans and ideas, often leading to unpredictable outcomes.

THE MAHOGANY MAFIA 3

"Fine. I'll be there, I said as the disconnect tone was in my ear." I was already bracing myself for whatever my father had in store.

As I hung up the phone, I couldn't shake the feeling that my father would bring both new opportunities and unforeseen challenges. Gring Joe's presence always stirred the pot, and in the volatile environment of Honduras, I knew firsthand that always meant trouble, for someone.

I landed in San Pedro Sula and drove to la Ceiba. I stood on the balcony above the Pharmacia Nueva once more, looking out past the church and at Pico Bonito and the jungle I used to sleep in. The sun had set, and darkness was creeping in. I knew that the days ahead would test my resilience and resolve in ways I hadn't yet imagined.

But if there was one thing I had learned from the 7th Special Forces, it was to face challenges quickly and with violence-of-action. With a deep breath, I steeled myself for the next chapter of my life, where the lines between business and survival would blur once again.

Chapter 2.   Hyper-Vigilance and IRC 936

When I got out of the Army, I was afraid. I had no idea what to do. Catherine was in love with me and looked at me for some sort of guidance. We loved Kentucky, so we decided to make that our permanent home. I was 26 years old and not well, though I tried to hide it. I knew that I needed to take care of my wife and I needed a career.

I saw an advertisement for a Career Fair one day and I went. I figured I was an ex-Army Officer, and had earned a couple of nice medals, surely I was hire-able material for someone. I ended up talking to the 1st person I saw when I walked through the door: Mr. Gatti, from Mr. Gatti's Pizza.

Mr. Gatti's Pizza was a locally owned family business that had been around for years. It was popular and busy and they needed someone to come in and manage the store for them. We negotiated my contract, it wasn't a whole lot, but it was a living and I became their new manager. I liked them a lot. I appreciated them taking a chance on me and giving me the opportunity, but after one too many people not showing up for their shifts, I realized that Mr. Gattis wasn't the place for me.

I needed to find an opportunity that would challenge my intellect and allow me to utilize all of the leadership and planning skills that I had developed and honed as an Officer. I figured I could get a job at some big company; make some decent money and Catherine and I would someday have a family.

"I think I need to go back to school. I've got so much more inside of me. I can't go work at another fast food place or anything like that."

"Do it. Nothing is holding you back. What do you want to pursue?"

Catherine was fully supportive of whatever I wanted to do, so the question was more of an "Okay, let's do it!"

"I'm going to get my M.B.A. from the University of Louisville."

It was settled. Just like that.

As fate would have it, the Dean of the Business school was a retired U.S. Air Force officer. Dean Taylor was a no-nonsense sort of guy who loved to offer tidbits about life and advice. He and I clicked immediately. I showed him, my picture on the cover of *Air Force Times* sitting in the middle of the Iraqi desert. He loved that picture.

"Character applies, honor does not."

I sat back to consider his words. I wasn't there just to make small talk and shoot the shit though. I had spent the previous days poring over the course guide. I had read everything about all of the classes and I had hatched my plan.

"Dean Taylor. I'd like to start with the Capstone Course."

"You are just as ambitious as I imagined you would be. But we can't do that. That class is for second-year students with a very keen idea of what they want to do."

"I understand. But I know what I want to do. I just need to figure it out."

"Which is precisely why you should begin with your normal coursework. It will only take you two years Adam. You'll be done in no time."

This was going to be a little bit harder than I thought.

"With all due respect Sir. You know what it takes to be an officer in the military. We have to be adept at everything that is required to lead and ensure that our men return home safely. If I take the capstone class first, it will help me understand what to pay attention to during every other course I take thereafter, it seems that you civilians got the training backwards."

This struck a chord. And I knew it. I put my arm on the cover of the Airforce magazine as a not-so-subtle piece of proof of my ability.

Dean Taylor signed off on my class selection and I began my pursuit of my M.B.A. with the hardest class that students must take to successfully earn their Master's. That was the Adam Rousselle way.

Catherine and I eked out our existence during this time. We were poor; I was a newly discharged soldier with very little money. We survived off love, cheap meals and a true need for stability in our lives. When school started in the Fall, she was just as excited as I was. We both knew that we were on our way.

"If you start your own business, you will get an A in all of these classes. This is the real reason why we are all here."

Those were the first words spoken by Professor Jeff Bracker in the Capstone Course at the University of Louisville. Bracker was a renowned and leading voice in Entrepreneurial Studies and his insight was pure brilliance. I got excited when I heard this. I had already done some research on him and knew that he was a molder of great businessmen and women.

"Here you are going to write your Business Plan. When you are done you will have the backbone for the endeavor that you have chosen to pursue."

I had questions, but I thought it was best to not ask them in class. Instead, I waited until everyone had left.

"Professor Bracker. When you say Business Plan. What exactly do you mean?"

He looked at me as if I had fallen out of a tree. I honestly didn't know. I had been a Soldier for my entire adult life up to that point. Thought I had sold Dean Taylor on my capabilities, I didn't know much about *business*.

"This is the Capstone Course you know. You're expected to know what a business Plan is by now."

"I know. I just got out of the Army, and I wanted to start with the most challenging classes."

"What was your rank?"

"First Lieutenant."

Bracker seemed slightly impressed.

"Where did you serve?"

"In the Gulf. First Squadron Seventh Calvary Regiment. Also spent time with the 7th Special Forces Group in Honduras."

"Honduras?" I could tell this *really* resonated with him.

"Okay, Mister Rousselle. Do some research on writing a Business Plan."

We departed and my mind was racing. I went home and read about the components of an effective Business Plan: Mission Statement. Barriers to entry. Competition. I engrossed myself in understanding the purpose of having a plan.

A few days later after class, Professor Bracker handed me U.S Code Title 26: The Internal Revenue Code Subtitle A Income Taxe, . book and told me "Find the tax codes for businesses."

This book was voluminous, and the writing was tiny at best. I hadn't figured out what my Business would be yet, so I knew that I would find it in this book.

I spent hours and nights tearing through the pages, ingesting paragraphs of seemingly useless details to many, but to me, it was as if I *had* to read every word on each page.

I didn't know it then, but this was a symptom of my undiagnosed Post Traumatic Stress Disorder (PTSD) called "hyper-vigilance." In a nutshell it meant that my mind could not settle down unless I read every detail of everything that I read. I listened to every word that came out of someone's mouth and I often took what they said too literally. I could not turn off this "obsession," and even if I could, I'm not sure I would've wanted to. It was the only way to try and forget the scenes from the War or those hours of preparation leading up to it.

Subconsciously I must've believed that if I kept my mind working, no matter how fatigued or delirious I may have become from sleep deprivation and mental stress, eventually I would figure out everything in the world I needed to know.

It all paid off. In my readings, I discovered Internal Revenue Code (IRC) 936, also known as the Possession Tax Credit. Section 936 was a provision in the U.S. tax code enacted in 1976 ostensibly to encourage business investment in Puerto Rico and other U.S. possessions. Congress voted to phase out Section 936 in 1996, citing excessive costs and the very limited number of U.S. companies that received the tax break and the Caribbean Basin Recovery Act (CBRA).

The CBRA had been set up by the United States to incentivize businesses to set up revenue-generating entities in Caribbean countries to boost their economies. These companies could operate in a U.S. Free Trade Zone where they would be afforded all of the resources they would receive in the United States while conducting business on foreign soil, except for one major factor: There was no corporate profit tax on certain imported items!

Bingo!

As I scrolled down the list of eligible countries and items for each country that were eligible for this, my heart pounded. I lined the list of acceptable products and BAM, there it was. *unfinished lumber - Honduras.*

I had found my business, but I needed clarification.

We discussed the CBRA in class the next day and I had to raise my hand and ask the question.

"Are you telling me that if I buy unfinished lumber in Honduras and come back to the U.S. and sell it for a million dollars, I don't have to pay taxes?'

"Yes."

That was all I needed to hear. I knew Honduras. I had contacts there. I had people there. I could walk anywhere in the country, and someone would've known me from my time that I was there before. This was meant for me and I was going to take full advantage of it. The only problem was that I didn't know shit about lumber.

I began to fervently research the lumber business and I learned that Brazil was the leading exporter of Mahogany wood. Brazil was much further away from the United States, so I knew that instantly my shipping cost would be cheaper. Brazilian companies operated from a high volume, low margin business approach. They relied on being able to ship tons of containers per week from Brazilian ports and made their money based on these massive shipments. I surmised that I needed to develop a low-volume, high-margin business to succeed. I wasn't going to be able to ship 150 containers a month. Hell, I didn't know how to ship 1 at this point, but I was sure as hell going to figure it out.

But that wasn't it. As fate would have it, as I was creating my Business Plan, Brazil issued a moratorium on the export of Mahogany lumber!

Un-believable! Nothing better could've happened to me. I was positioning myself to become the only supplier of Mahogany in the world.

Once I had gotten my preliminary data together, I picked up the phone to call my Dad. He was going to be integral in this business if it was going to succeed and I needed him to be on board. I only had a landline, so I called the base in Honduras and the Operator answered.

"I need a patch to 420831.:

I knew that she had to patch me through. No one else knew what to say or how to contact the Operator unless they had the right to do so. I reasoned the Army wouldn't mind that a former soldier was trying to better himself.

She gladly patched me through and Dad answered in his usual cheerful tone.

"Heeeyyy."

"Dad we're going into the lumber business."

"Great."

"What do you know about Mahogany?"

"Nothing."

Neither of us had a clue, but the deeper I delved into my Business Plan that all began to change.

Chapter 3.   All Or Nothing

I compiled data and information for months. Through my research for my Business Plan, I learned that there is a major difference between Brazilian Mahogany and Honduras Mahogany. By industry standards, Honduran Mahogany was considered more exotic and thus carried a higher value.

Honduran Mahogany had more silica. These tiny black dots of silica essentially lubricated the saw blades and meant that it was easier to cut. It would also allow for the wood to be shaped into fine furniture and other items easier. From a manufacturing standpoint, this meant that Honduran Mahogany would retain its shape better. It wouldn't chip. It wouldn't defect like all the other types of lumber would.

This was important to me because if my potential customers were going to be manufacturing lumber on the regular basis, in order to keep costs down and make greater profits, they needed to be able to get the full usage out of the blades on their saws. If for example they had Brazilian Mahogany (though I couldn't get any at that point) and Honduran Mahogany and all my blades were exactly the same sharpness, they would need to sharpen their blades more when cutting Brazilian wood as opposed to Honduran.

This would mean that it would take more time, which would drive up labor costs and eat into their bottom line, which would then adversely affect their willingness to work with me at my prices.

But that wasn't all.

Because it's softer, Honduran wood takes a better *patina* which meant it would darken with more sun rather than age, than the Brazilian because of the... silica!

In other words, Honduran Mahogany was *perfect*

This was the science behind lumber, and I gorged myself with learning all that I could. I loved the "why" things were the way that were. I loved understanding what made things the way that were. My hyper-vigilance only increased my appetite for information.

"Do you think you can manage the logistics of the business?"

"Sure thing Son."

THE MAHOGANY MAFIA

"That's going to require you to manage our team down in Honduras."

"I know people."

I knew my Dad knew people. That was one of the main reasons we were on the phone. We talked like this for months trying to put it all together in my plan and then finally, it was done.

When I completed my Business Plan, CBI International launched the same day. We were officially in the lumber business.

I knew a lot about the science of lumber, but I didn't know anything about *who* to sell it to and *how* to do it. But I wasn't afraid to make a mistake. So, I did what everyone did back in 1992 before the internet and instant information gathering: I picked up the phone and began calling.

I just wanted to talk to people who sold lumber. I needed insight and connections.

I called up 84 Lumber.

"Hey do you guys buy Mahogany?"

You would've thought I asked the guy if he knew how to do an appendectomy.

"No. Are you kidding me? We sell two by fours."

I called up Home Depot

"Do you sell Mahogany?"

"Ma what? No. Who is this?"

Click.

I tried Lowe's, fully anticipating hearing the "click" again.

"Well, we have it as a specialty item, but maybe two loads a year."

It was a start.

Then I called local saw mills. The answer was always the same.

"No, I just cut local trees from the local forests" type thing.

Then one day I called a sawmill and I got the break that I needed.

"I know a guy who does all of that plus some exotics."

12 ★ ADAM ROUSSELLE

Technically Honduran Mahogany was not an "*exotic*" but for them anything not found somewhere in the local forests and mountains qualified.

I was thrilled beyond words.

Koetter Woodworking was in Starlight, Indiana, which was only about 20 miles from Louisville. It was a family-owned business that had been started by Tom Koetter about 40 years earlier.

I called and asked to speak to Tom.

"Tom, how are you? Adam Rousselle. Would you be interested in purchasing Honduran Mahogany at a great price?."

"You don't' have Mahogany. Stop bullshittin' me."

"I absolutely do. I can get as much of it as you want."

I'm not sure what that meant. I didn't know how much of it I could actually get, but I knew that there was a shitload of it in Honduras and I was the only one who had access to it.

"What do you know about Honduran Mahogany?"

"I know that Brazil has a moratorium on the export of Mahogany and I am the only person in the world who can get it right now."

"How long have you been in business?"

"Just getting started but we plan on being here for a while, Sir."

"Sir? You an ex-military man?"
"Yessir. Army."

"I'll tell you what Adam Rousselle. I will take a truckload of Honduran Mahogany at market price."

"Great!"

What the was the market price?

I searched and discovered that the market rates were published every Monday morning in the Hardwood Market Report. This report was vital to any lumber business. As I thumbed through, I flipped it over and saw an ad for a company called "Robinson's Lumber" in New Orleans. Their ad mentioned that they specialized in Brazilian Mahogany as well as many other species of wood. It was owned by a man named Toto.

When I got Toto on the phone I told him the truth.

"Mr. Robinson and I need your help."

He had a thick Louisiana accent that gave away his Cajun roots instantly. He was warm and friendly as many Southerners I had encountered to that point were.

"What's going on?"

I told him I had Honduran Mahogany and he was fascinated.

"Oh yeah?"

"I want to get this thing started in Honduras."

"My father tried to export Mahogany from Honduras forty years ago and they almost killed him."

I wasn't going to be deterred, but Toto wasn't trying to scare me off. He was just telling me the truth.

"These guys are going to give you dead-green lumber. You pay for it. They're going to cut it down and give it to you."

He seemed to lean into the phone to make sure that I was listening.

"But understand Adam, because its dead-green, it can perish. It's like a vegetable. The tree is alive and dead. The center is dead. The outside has a sap ring along the outside of the tree. Depending on the time of year the sap goes up and down. In the sap is a form of glucose that feeds the plant. That sugar is being manufactured by the root system which creates a chemical reaction with the earth. That's how it's made. So, if you take a tree and cut it down and don't take the sap away the sap will degrade and when it does it will stain the lumber that it touches and cut its value in half. Nobody wants stained lumber."

I hung on to Toto's every word, furiously taking notes . This was invaluable information that may have taken me months to understand.

The truth is what Toto did for me was truly remarkable. In theory, I was his competitor; trying to infringe on his market. He was the biggest importer of Brazilian Mahogany in the country, and he could've easily just brushed me off. But he didn't. He chose to share his wisdom and insight with me with no strings attached. Of course, my business would never be able to compete with him, because he was shipping 130 containers a week, but still the gesture was so genuine and kind that I felt indebted to him.

He left me with the crux of the whole thing.

"Nobody wants a sap ring in their lumber products. You can't manufacture anything with it. You have to cut it off."

Sap was bad. I understood that.

I called my Dad and told him I wanted to buy a truckload of Mahogany.

"How much goes into a truck?"

I had no clue.

I then had to learn about what kind of truck we needed. I had to learn about the weight of the truck. I didn't want a tractor-trailer. I needed a corrugated container. 40 or 48 feet? Damned if I knew. What's the difference? One's 40 one's 48 feet long. They weight out the same. You can either cube out or weight out. It needed to cube out or you can only put so much weight in there.

What was the specific weight of Mahogany? I didn't know and of course Dad didn't. Air dried? Kiln dried or Dead Green? I didn't know.

Dad and I bounced these questions around for weeks. In the end we didn't really have a satisfactory answer to any of the questions but we did know one thing.

"Make sure none of the trees have any sap. It will ruin the whole god damned shipment!"

When I was discharged from the Army, I was given $38,000 as my medical discharge and told "Good Luck." We lived off of that money. It was all the money that Catherine and I had.

When I went to the bank to withdraw $30,000 of what we had left, I could feel a pit in my stomach. In a few hours I would be on a plane to Honduras to go and pay some guys that I had never met, that Dad had found, every penny to my name. If this failed, I wasn't sure what I would do.

"Here."

Dad tossed me a pistol as we climbed into an off-road jeep. I was not afraid of guns. I was accustomed to guns. Everyone had guns, so it was almost a part of the clothes you put on that day.

"Pants. Shirt. Socks. Gun."

THE MAHOGANY MAFIA 15

I clutched the briefcase holding the money next to me. Dad had brought two of his friends with him. Of course they had guns too.

We drove for a couple of hours outside of the city and into the mountains. It was just before sunset and already getting dark. The insanity of what we were about to do was beyond my comprehension. I trusted my Dad. I knew that he knew; where we were going and who we were talking to. I also felt confident in my own abilities. I had been to war.

We arrived at a hut off the side of the dirt road. A generator rumbled just to the side, powering an air conditioner. I wondered if I had sold whoever was in that hut, that generator when I was trading things in the Army.

Two armed guards huddled outside, smoking a cigarette. I could tell there were others in the shadow. No one really said anything. They half-smiled when they saw us walking up.

"Que Pasa?"

I greeted them with a smile. They smiled back, but their eyes dropped down to the black briefcase I gripped tightly.

We walked into the hut and sat down at a table as a light overhead danced from the air of the air conditioner. Four men walked in, and a chubby Honduran man smiled.

"Gringo Joe." He and Dad shook hands and I set the briefcase on top of the table as the men sat down. I put my pistol in front of me on the table too for everyone to see.

The Chubby Man smiled playfully.

The amount of money in that briefcase was equivalent to millions in America. It could have changed the trajectory of a family for generations. My life's savings (or earnings) would have been like winning the lottery. I slid the briefcase to the Man, and he opened it.

"That's a lot of money. It can help a lot of people here in your village. If you do right by me, there will be plenty more of where that came from. You can kill me now and that money will be gone."

I looked all of them in the eyes. Dad smiled. It was a tense moment and then the Chubby Man and everyone else cracked a smile.

"We have a deal."

He sounded like an overworked game show host who had just been told his show was canceled.

"Now we celebrate."

One of the guards put four liquor bottles on the table. The chubby man poured drinks for me and my Dad. The others poured their own.

"To Gringo Joe."

It took three months for that container to finally reach me in Louisville. It had stayed in Miami for an extra 3 weeks because Customs had to search it for drugs. Honduras was a major drug exporter to the U.S. at that time and they did everything they could, short of sawing the lumber in half to make sure there weren't any drugs inside of the wood itself.

When I got the news that I could come and get the container, I was ecstatic. I had rented a truck to drive it up to Koetter. In Indiana. As I rode up the freeway, I felt good. In just a few short months I had gone from idea to reality and was about to go and make a shitload of money for a minimal amount of work. I let the windows down and hung my arm out of the window as I drove through the rolling Indiana farmland.

Things were about to change.

When I pulled into the lumber yard, Tom, who was in his 60s, and his son, Jerry came out to greet me. I swelled with pride as I shook their hands.

"We didn't think you were going to come through."

"Yeah. I've got another one on the way. I know you're going to like this."

"Well let's see it."

Jerry motioned to the back of the container.

I hustled back and threw it open. Jerry and Tom eyeballed the wood and instantly my heart sank. Their surprised expressions quickly shifted to disgusted scowls right before my eyes.

"What the hell is this? This is garbage."

Jerry was ready to kick me out of the yard. I had wasted their time and time was money for these guys.

"What do you mean?"

I did not understand the problem.

The lumber had been sawed right out of the woods (which apparently it shouldn't have been) and it was just stacked right on top of each other.

"Where are the six quarters? The half-quarters? Four quarters?"

"I'm sorry I don't know what you mean."

I learned later that everything was based on quarters. 8 quarters meant 8/4 or 2 inches. 4/4 quarter meant 1 inch and so forth. Koetter never gave me any specifications and I didn't know to ask.

My wood had been cut into whatever size they wanted.

Jerry called out to his men to come over. They shut down the factory right there. Tom put his hand to his head and wiped the imaginary sweat away. I felt like the dog that had just shitted on his Persian Rug.

What I didn't know then, out of sheer ignorance was that when you ship lumber you bundle it together so that it can get taken off with a forklift. The dudes in Honduras just packed it one on top of the next. The only way to get this lumber out was by hand. It was going to take 40 guys 2 hours to offload this truck.

And the lumber was dead-green!

It had mold all over it. It was full of water, and it was like 1000 degrees inside of that container. In his kindness, Toto forgot to tell me I had to separate each board from the next. This fiasco was going to cost Koetter a fortune of lost opportunity manufacturing.

"Just do it for him."

Tom looked at Jerry and walked away. Just like that. He had decided right there that he would eat the cost of this to help me out. He wanted to keep his word that they would pay for whatever they could use.

Jerry didn't bat an eye. He got his guys working on unloading the container. All I could do was stand and watch.

Jerry took me aside and he showed me how green it was.

"All of this lumber is sap-stained. It's ruined. It's two common. It probably has a value of about 30 percent of what you paid for it. We're going to keep our promise. But I don't think you're going to get anything out of this."

"Jerry I don't mind losing. I don't want to take too much of your time. What should I have done? Show me what you're looking for please."

"See that right there?" Jerry pointed to a bundle of wood in their yard.

"That's a bundle of Mahogany. If you bundle it, it won't have that problem. Every single piece of wood you have has that mold on it."

He pointed to the container.

"I've got 16 quarter and 4 quarter in the same truck."

"You said you will take whatever."

"Yeah, but I don't mean this."

Jerry studied the wood as it came off of the truck. I snapped pictures with my portable Polaroid camera.

Click. Roll. Click. Roll.

It was one of those ones that you could throw away once the film was done.

"I'll kiln dry it for you and after that, we'll grade it."

I drove home a shell of the man I was. I thought for sure I would get a big check that day when they got this shipment of rare Honduran Mahogany. Instead, I was going home broke, hoping that I would get some good news soon.

I came back a month later and he gave me the lowest price on earth.

"$6,000. I don't think it's Mahogany. Mine looks blondish and yours looks red.:"

I assured him it was Mahogany.

He grabbed some of the wood and cut two boards. When he cut them they came out identical.

"Wow, I was wrong." He inspected the boards. "It is Mahogany, but it looks different."

Just like that!

"We're going to clean it off. The Kiln process kills the mold." Your lumber looks great.

THE MAHOGANY MAFIA 19

As he continued planing the boards we , saw that the planer blade had been chipping out the curly-grained. That was rare. I looked at all the lumber behind it.

"Stop. Can we put this aside?"

They put that bundle of wood to the side.

They brought out the next bundle. It was similar and I asked him to put that aside for me. We did this until I had a pickup truck load of wood that seemed to be "bad.:

Jerry gave me $18,000 for the wood he kept.

"Come back when you get some more."

I excitedly drove home. I didn't get all our money back, but I had a whole pickup truck worth of something rare. "Someone will want this," I kept telling myself.

I did some research and sure enough the Mahogany that I had was Full Bubble Tight Curl Quilted Mahogany. It came from the trunks of trees that grew on the inclines along the rivers in Honduras. The sloping and the moisture created a natural pattern unlike anything else in the world. It was the most valuable lumber of our species on the planet and no one had had it in 20 years. Like the "Beverly Hill Billies," I had just struck gold!

I called high-end dealers around the country to let them know what I had. A guy from California flew out to Louisville and bought 1 *board* for $2,000. Just one board.

"All you have to do is call me. I'll buy it."

He was serious and I knew he was.

A guy from Berea Hardwoods in Ohio asked me to ship me a piece as proof. I cut a 12-inch piece of the board and shipped it to him. When he got it, he called me yelling.

"You're an idiot." You should've never cut this off the board. The longer it is the more value it has. How much of this do you have?"

"I got a pickup truck full."

"No you don't."

Things were picking up. I had developed this unspoken mantra that I used daily; "Are you a buyer or a liar?" I thought of asking this guy the question out loud.

"I'll drive it to you and you can get it if you don't believe me."

I sold every piece of that shipment off of my pickup truck and made $25,000.

We got our money back and then some.

Chapter 4. The Return Of Gringo Joe

No one expected me to be able to pull off getting a container of lumber from Honduras to the United States. That was a major international feat that required coordination of several moving parts. The overall thinking was "This young, Vet just couldn't make it happen." The Koetters didn't expect me to be able to get a permit from the Department of Agriculture to allow me to bring in a container. No one imagined I would be able to actually get the shipment to the dock in Honduras, let alone to Starlight, Indiana without some sort of major mistake.

We proved them all wrong.

Logistically we had pulled off the coup and I knew that the questions would start.

"Can you do it again?"

I went back to visit Tom Koetter. If I wanted to make a splash in the market, I needed him to be on board.

"Seems like the only problem that we have is lumber grade, Mr. Koetter."

I had prepared my notes for our meeting and was ready to state my case for another shipment.

"My lumber is thirty percent cheaper. Your margins are two percent. In your best year, you may make six and a half percent."

Tom Koetter leaned back in his chair with his hands folded behind his head. His expression, screamed, "You're treading on thin ice kid."

But I was too focused and ignorant to care. I didn't know I had stepped on his toes. I thought I was doing him a favor by pointing this out to him. I had studied Koetter's business and financials. I knew everything about their operation, because as I saw it, I had to make a case for why he would want to do business with me.

The fact is, no one wants someone to come in and talk to them about their business's profits and margins. That's sacred information and I imagine I kind of pissed Tom Koetter off by doing it.

But he let me continue, despite his clear disdain for my prying.

"What if I could bring the lumber here and you had a grader at my mill? What if every time I shipped it, you could sell it before it arrived. What if we could ship it somewhere else?"

These were big "what ifs" I didn't have a mill, nor did we have the capacity yet to talk about shipping lumber all over the place. But I knew if Tom Koetter wanted it, I could figure out a way to make this all happen.

"I'm not in the lumber resell business son."

I couldn't be deterred. I could sense I was close.

"If my math is right about the delivery, it will only take 3 weeks. If I could do it and do it that fast, would it be profitable?"

"Absolutely."

"Let's give it a go then."

Koetter thought for a moment. The deal is he didn't really *need* my lumber. He had a yard of the stuff that was nearly enough to build a small country. His decision was less about lumber and more about *me*.

"Give me another one."

We shook hands and the deal was done.

Tom Koetter liked me.

I had work to do. I was confident in our ability to figure out the logistics and coordination of the actual shipments. I was not remotely confident that Dad would not potentially send a batch of lumber that I might not be able to sell.

Tom Koetter had done me a tremendous favor by giving me even a chance to check my notes (that old green notebook that I wrote everything down in) and realize that our wood was just like theirs. I got lucky once, and I knew it wasn't going to happen again with any other company.

I had managed to salvage our reputation, by unloading the wood, but we weren't going to be able to exist like that.

When I got back to my office I called my father on a patch from Palmerola AFB..

"It won't happen again."

THE MAHOGANY MAFIA

"You're right it's not going to happen again, because I'm not going to let you mess it up again."

I was livid. I was the one that was at risk financially and had to face the embarrassment and stares from the Koetters and their men on the lumber yard. Dad tried to brush it off, which only further infuriated me.

"Calm down Adam. I will handle it. The lumber sold. Everything is good."

"That's not business Dad! That was my entire life's savings! Not yours. Mine!"

"Did you sell everything that you had?"

"Most of it."

"Did you get your money back?"

"That's not the point."

Dad had this way of being really good at spending other people's money and making everyone feel like things were perfect. He had been a hustler and transient for most of his life. He didn't mind living on the edge. He had this way of always making things seem like they were fine, because for him they always were. Most of his business ventures had worked until they didn't, and he relied on his belief that he would get through anything. He saw the world through rose-colored glasses that never changed.

As far as I could tell, he hadn't told the guys in Honduras anything about our shipment. He probably figured that it didn't really matter to them.

Like hell it didn't.

"I'm coming down there."

I had decided that I couldn't spend another penny unless I went down to Honduras and saw the wood for myself. Before it was shipped. We weren't going to have a repeat performance.

I took some banding clips and a bander with me to Honduras as Dad had requested. We hadn't moved into a free trade zone facility yet, but the city of La Ceiba had allowed us to operate out of an abandoned plant on the edge of the city. As I stepped out into the yard, I immediately noticed two things: 1. There was a giant pig cooking on a smoker on the far end of the yard. The aroma was intoxicating, and my stomach grumbled. And 2. There was a massive pile of lumber at one end of the yard. It could've been a quarter of a football field and it was piled up 30 feet in the air.

"Who the hell is going to clean that up?"

I thought to myself when I saw that pile. It was going to be a real headache for someone.

I found Dad sitting with his arms folded across his big belly in the warm Honduran morning. He watched his men using the bander and band rings that I brought with me, with a satisfied look on his face. I was still a little peeved about the wood incident and ready to go for round 2 with my Dad about it.

"Who's shit is that?"

I pointed to the massive pile of what looked like pixie sticks that took up all of the space.

"That's all of the shit I rejected."

He looked at me with a knowing grin.

"What do you mean?"

"After we talked, I changed up how we were doing business around here. That is all the shit that I told them we couldn't use. If I saw as much as a blemish on the baby's ass I threw it out."

I allowed that to sink in for a moment.

He had listened to me.

I thought that he hadn't told the men about the screwed up lumber, but I was wrong. But not only did he tell them about it, he established a standard in our operations that would prove vital to our future success. He set the standard and created a physical reminder for everyone. "I'm not taking shit again." Just at the right moment, he told everyone exactly what happened.

Dad had 5 loads of lumber left in his yard and the guys who brought it had begged him to take it. It would take forever for them to reload their trucks and then take that wood somewhere and dump it. So he haggled with them for a while, until eventually those guys *begged* Dad to take the lumber.

"This shit is worthless!:

Eventually, they *gave* him all of that lumber.

Dad just left the lumber there. He could've put it aside and probably gone through and found more good pieces than bad pieces in that pile, but he did something far smarter: he let it sit outside and get wet.

Every time someone brought a truck of lumber, he would scoff,

"Are you bringing me some more of that shit?"

He would then point at the pile in the yard.

No one wanted to bring that in. They knew that Gringo Joe was the money guy, and they did not want him to get cut off from the money. When he arrived, he told them,

"This is the fucking boss. We can't give him that shit again."

When the first shipment happened, the guys would bring the wood to Dad and just throw it off the truck. He took this opportunity to instill a lesson in them all. If you were throwing wood off the truck and it went in that pile, then you know you had screwed up and you could potentially not get paid again.

He told the guys that they had to stack the wood neatly. This was a big deal. It taught these guys to have some respect for the wood that they were bringing to us. They would want to make sure that it was quality. They would want to make sure that it was treated properly. They should want to ensure that they were doing the best for Gringo Joe because he always did that for them.

These men looked at Dad as if he was their goal. He was well over 340 pounds now and in their country being fat meant being wealthy. To them, Gringo Joe might be the richest man they would meet in their lives.

Dad for his part helped foster this idea by doing things like buying an entire hog and feeding everyone there without ever eating any of it himself.

They quickly learned that fat Gringo Joe would take care of them if they took care of him.

I could only sit back in admiration as I watched Dad feed those guys that day. They loved being around. We were working on our 2nd shipment to Koetter and more were on the horizon.

Dad knew that there was value in that lumber, but he left it there for months. He never wanted them to think that he had outmaneuvered or manipulated them.

Eventually, he told the guys "We have to cut this into something" and we shipped most of it for sale.

Tom Sawyer had arrived in Honduras.

I was satisfied with what I saw and now I needed to get busy.

I had to go and get real money. Bank money. Risk money. Oh my God lose your ass money and I wasn't going to do anything unless I saw it myself. First step: work on the details.

We don't have the free zone lined up yet.

The company grew. The next shipment was 2 trucks. It was absolutely a different operation.

Shipping one container at a time and selling it to Koetter was not an effective or successful business model. Sure, it worked, but it was only going to be a nickel and dime operation and it simply going to be worth it.

We needed cash and we needed it quickly.

Actually, we needed something that was even better than cash. Something that I had never really had before in my life and never quite understood. It was the thing that was as American as Apple Pie and just as sweet…

… We needed credit.

As an Army Vet, I instantly had great credit. People wanted to do business with ex-soldiers for the same reason, Toto Robinson and Tom Koetter were willing to trust me and work with me; they knew that we would keep our word and do what we said. It was that simple.

I leveraged my good credit to get a loan from PNC Bank in Kentucky. We needed to purchase equipment, some sort of warehouse facility, and numerous incidentals like metal bands to hold the lumber together to get started. I had a strong business plan that I had written, and my financial calculations were on point. It was undeniable.

"We need a house."

Catherine and I came to the same conclusion almost simultaneously. I had been thinking about it for months and so had she. Apartment living was okay, but we had just started our own company! I named it CBI Lumber International, Inc. CBI stood for the Caribbean Basin Initiative Section 936 of the IRS Tax Code. CBI was about to explode. We envisioned hosting friends and family for big dinner parties and cookouts, while also having enough room to walk around in the kitchen together. We needed an upgrade, ASAP.

We drove around searching for the right place. We looked at several homes that we thought we might be able to afford (I had credit out the wazoo so I wasn't worried), but nothing caught our eye. That is until we found this empty corner lot on the first green of the Pine Vally Golf Course in Elizabethtown, Kentucky.

"That's it!"

Catherine was excited, which made me excited. We talked about how we imagined our home would look and that was it. Just like that.

I met Ed Hawkins that year. Ed seemed to be the most socially and financially successful gentleman in the region. He was kind, polite and gracious to Catherine and I. For the few moments I did have with him, I knew we would be friends.

I applied for a VA loan which I got, and we made a decision to build our home ourselves, while also building our business! That's the beauty of being young and adventurous/ You have no idea what you're doing, but you go ahead and do it anyway.

Dad and I had built houses in Florida, but I'm not sure that designated me as a "builder." It didn't' matter though. I was going to do it.

Armed with my newfound stellar credit, we began purchasing materials for our home and business.

The first thing that I had to do was make sure I separated my personal assets from the company. We needed some sort of operation in the states to set the bank's mind at ease. It's nearly impossible to get a U.S. Bank or investors to put money into an entity that is solely based in a foreign country.

Catherine and I hired Geoff Pinkerton, Jerry Renneker, Ange Deaton, and Ilka Matzke. We rented a small warehouse from our friend Kevin at a small distribution yard in Elizabethtown KY. These were mostly friends, whom we trusted and knew would help us be successful. We were a small operation with tons of potential business, but we had a ways to go.

Down in Honduras, good ol' Gringo Joe put together his consigliere. He tapped Jimmy Malone to run operations and security for us. Jimmy was the coolest guy. He had this hearty laugh that you could hear from miles away. His voice was high pitched, and he wore a bright smile constantly.

Jimmy was of Afro-Caribbean descent, with dark skin and bright white teeth and his King's English accent was amazing. He and Dad had been friends for years and Jimmy spoke the language of the people. Not just Spanish, but the *language* He was fearless and friendly until someone pissed him off. He carried a big 45-caliber pistol on his hip everywhere he went. There was no doubt that he would shoot someone and in later years he would say it. People generally avoided seeing the bad side of Jimmy.

Dad got Hernan Leva to run our Finance Department. This guy was a master of numbers. I used to think he was some kind of savant or something. He had worked in banking for years and like everyone else, Dad came in contact with, he loved Gringo Joe. I felt at ease knowing that Hernan was around.

Dad enlisted his buddy John Salazar to handle daily mill operations. We needed someone who knew what he was doing with the lumber and could make sure that it was being cut, packed, and shipped correctly. John needed training in the operation of different saws and mills in the coming months and we made sure to keep him well-versed in the machines. He was a mechanical guy who could fix anything.

Dad also hired a guy named Alex to be a key manager at the plant. Alex was a hard read. He was a drifter, and we never really got a good sense of where he was from. I wasn't sure how I felt about Alex. There was something that I just couldn't put my finger on. Dad trusted him though and that's all that mattered then.

Finally, there was Luis. Luis was Gringo Joe's driver and bodyguard. Plain and simple. He was a handsome, portly, red-head of Anglo Saxon and Honduran ancestry who seemed to stand out from everyone else in Honduras. He was short in stature, but his shadow was long and intimidating to some.

Dad trusted Luis with his life. And so did I. He was unabashedly loyal and trustworthy, and Dad needed a man like Luis in his corner.

Like Jimmy, Luis always carried a gun. Unlike Jimmy though, Luis also always had a shovel. No one asked about his shovel and I'm not sure he would've told us anyways. But I think we all had our assumptions, and we all knew, no one was to mess with Gringo Joe when Luis was around. And no one *ever* crossed Luis." Luis had this constant smile on his face though. You weren't sure what he was thinking. He just smiled and looked after Gringo Joe.

I didn't choose any of these folks and I figured it was best that Dad picked his own operations team. I had enough things on my plate already and I knew that he would surround himself with the right people. I got on the phone and started calling everyone. Business was about to boom.

Chapter 5. The Best No Chicken Money

The second shipment went off without a hitch and we started rolling. I made 100 calls a day to every exotic lumber vendor I could find around the world.

"Hey… This is Adam…"

I talked so much to so many people that I would be hoarse at night, and then get up and do it all over again.

And I loved it.

I was calling and trying to rig up a fax machine before fax machines were even standard to contact people. They couldn't believe that we could get this stuff.

"How much can you get?"

"As much as you want."

"How fast can you get it here?"

"When do you need it?"

I didn't say "No." Ever. We could pull this all off.

Down in Honduras, we needed a place for a sawmill which could qualify as a Free Zone manufacturing site. We applied and were accepted into the La Ceiba abandoned Standard Oil Rail Yard! This meant that we had zero limitations on the amount of lumber that we could manufacture and we were protected under an agreement between the United States and Honduras.

This wasn't all that I had to juggle however.

In the middle of launching and international business, Catherine and I were building a house.

With the money from my VA loan, I brought supplies and started the building process myself. Of course we had contractors, who were mostly referrals from friends, doing some of the work, but most of it was Catherine and I doing it ourselves. I had learned a few things from Dad down in Florida about building homes, so I wasn't a complete novice.

I needed to get some lumber one day and ran to the local Lowe's in Elizabethtown. I had seen that they were offering a discount on the wood and building supplies, so I decided I would stock up on everything. I had lots of cash from my VA loan so I literally bought the house.

When I got up to pay, there was a problem.

"We can't give you a discount on all of that. It's only up to $1000."

"What do you mean? This is my purchase and I came here specifically because of the discount." I had the ad with me and knew what it said.

"I understand Sir. But this exceeds our limit."

This made no sense to me, and I really didn't have the time to waste going back and forth with the Clerk. I pleaded my case. She stated hers. Finally, I asked to see a manager. I refused to leave without getting the advertised discount; regardless of how much of a time crunch I may have been under.

"Hi. Mister Rousselle. I'm Al Lenarden." We shook hands and I instantly liked this guy. I had always been good at reading people and Al's demeanor was warm and welcoming from the start.

Al took a moment to listen to my side of the story. We reviewed the ad together and sure enough I was right. There was no mention of a limit. He advised the Clerk to honor the discount for my entire purchase and then he and I began to talk.

"You're in the lumber business?"

And just like that, a friendship was forged.

I bought all our lumber and home construction supplies from the Lowe's store and we built a strong and lasting friendship.

Dad knew that we would need lumber and lots of it. He started making deals with local truckers to enlist more help. Companies wanted to buy our lumber, but it wasn't that simple.

"We won't get paid for 45 days. Do you think these guys will wait?"

"Fuck no. They'll kill us all."

Dad was emphatic with his answer.

I was leveraging relationships, my credit, and my reputation to build our business, but it didn't eliminate one of our main issues. Cash flow was real a problem for us. We needed real, "put your ass on the line" type money to operate, otherwise the trucks would stop driving which meant the lumber would stop arriving, which meant that customers would never get their products and our reputation would be ruined forever.

So in the midst of building our home, Catherine and I hopped on a flight to Honduras.

We met with Judy Salazaar, a SVP at Banco Atlantida in La Ceiba. Judy was a friendly and nice woman, who seemed to understand our plight. She was willing to help and she did, but it would come with a hefty price that I couldn't see coming at the time.

To be fair, I don't even know if Judy knew the ramifications of her involvement with me. But that's hindsight and at the time, she was a lifesaver.

We thanked her and went about the business of growing CBI.

Now that we had our site at the old rail yard, we needed sawmills to do our cutting at the yard. I researched various types of mills.

Circle sawmills were used for logs. Their blades were 1/4" thick and created a ton of waste. However, we only received "cants" which were essentially odd shaped blocks of wood 4-6 inches thick, 6-10 feet long and 6-12 inches wide.

This was the only way we could get the wood from the jungle to a pickup point to bring it to our yard. Those cants had to be placed on the backs of mules and led down a road from the jungle that overlooked steep cliffs and traversed through narrow passageways.

Mules were used because the footing was unsteady, and horses would have fallen to their deaths on those ledges. It was a slow and tedious process, but it was the only way it could be done.

I did the calculations and realized that putting a 1/4" saw blade on a 5" thick board and cutting it into 4 pieces would lose 4 x 1/4" or 20% of the wood. That was just throwing away money that we couldn't' afford to lose.

I studied what mills could do better and decided on a band sawmill. The blades were "thin kerf" and 1/8" thick. I traveled to Indiana and bought our first Wood Miser sawmill.

I put it on a boat along with a new Chevy 250 diesel truck with a 5th wheel and trailer and sent it to Dad right away and we were in business. We could haul our sawmill to our new yard and pick up wood with our 5th wheel trailer.

The drive was 6 hours long from the mill to the wood. It wasn't possible to feed the mill with our truck.

We made a deal with more local truckers and their families. You bring the wood, we pay on delivery. And boy did we pay. The trucks started arriving nonstop to keep our mill running 24 hours a day. This was good for inventory and for business (I was selling my ass off now). But we had to let our staff sleep. We hired more staff with Dad and John's direction, and I sent John Salazar to Indiana to be trained by the Wood Mizer company.

When he was done, I bought 3 more mills.

Back in the states, I hired my old buddy Michael Reiber from the Army to help me with sales. I was calling every exotic lumber company in the world, and they were taking my calls. The thing was the more lumber and trees we cut, the more we began to discover more exotic species of lumber. In addition to our Mahogany, we began to acquire Lignum Vitae, Coco Bolo and Honduran Rosewood. We were like the miners in the 1800s in the United States, discovering gold in the mountains and rivers of the West.

World Timber, which was based in North Carolina asked us to fax them our quotes. They were a major supplier to everyone around the world and we needed to be in business with them. It never made sense to me that whatever we shipped always had to go through North Carolina before it got anywhere else in the United States. The wood would leave Honduras, end up in Charleston, South Carolina on a ship, and then get railed to Hickory, North Carolina. Everything went through these guys, and they had heard about us and wanted to be involved with us.

My old buddy Tom Koetter was sending business our way too.

"Adam, send quilted mahogany to Luther's Mercantile second day air and mail the photos to Mario Messina."

"Done."

Our lumber yard in Honduras was bursting at the seams. It was like a sea of red quilted Mahogany everywhere. Dad constantly needed supplies and I was constantly hustling to get them to him.

"Adam, we need more trucks."

"Okay."

I'd go and buy more trucks and get them on Seaboard and off to Honduras in a couple of days.

Dad needed Paraffin. I shipped it. Wax. It's on the way. Trucks, wax and paraffin. Done deal. I became a Master shipper in between calls with potential new clients in Korea.

But that wasn't all.

When the World Timber meeting came to the University of Louisville I did research with my professor Jeff Bracker and presented at the meeting. It was all exhausting, but I loved every moment of it. I was building that stability that I needed and longed for, for Catherine and It felt good to know that I was doing something that no one in the world believed I or anyone could do. I had come a long way from my days back in my hometown, Mechanicville New York, where I sometimes didn't have enough food to eat or clothes that fit.

Still the business came with many challenges and for us the constant was always cash flow.

We were in a constant state of "robbing Peter to pay Paul." Dad and I weren't making any money personally per se. Everything that we earned had to go back into the business. It was strictly me continuously leveraging my relationships to get the things that I needed.

But that shit didn't matter to the guys in Honduras who needed their cash on time. I knew that no matter what happened, Dad needed to have cash, and lots of it at any given moment.

There's a publication that banks use when deciding on whether to give a loan to company called Robert Morris and Associates Guide to Industry Standards. What this book does is essentially give you the exact ratios and guidelines for how much money a business should be making at various points in its lifetime. This helps determine risk and likelihood of full repayment. If a business falls too far below the industry standard for that business, then obviously that's a high-risk business and the bank will probably decline to make the loan. The same applies on the opposite end. If a company makes *too much* money on their financial statements, then there's a likelihood that they're either fudging the books or the business is booming and likely won't be around long.

We were booming, but we had every idea of being around for many years to come. Still when Hogue Grips, a high-end grip maker for knives and guns wanted to do business with us, we didn't have the money to fill their particular order. I needed to request another note from PNC Bank and I needed to make sure that my numbers hit the sweet spot.

THE MAHOGANY MAFIA

After hours of research and evaluations of our accounting records and subsequent reconciliations with the Robert Morris and Associates Industry averages, I secured more financial money for CBI!

But it wasn't enough.

It was a band-aid on a gaping wound that required full treatment.

All of that was soon to change though.

In the late fall of 1993, Kentucky experienced what was called "the 100 year snowstorm." It was unbelievable. In just a day, snow blanketed most of the state and much of the Eastern part of the country. This sucked for me because I had secured a potential buyer for 98,000 pounds of Lignum Vitae from Honduras. I had spoken with Peter Weise of Theodor Nagle Timber in Germany who was a major player in the industry. We hit it off quickly, but he did not believe that I could get that much of the Honduran exotic.

"Not only can I get it, but I will have it there in Kentucky for you to see."

I could make this bold statement by the time I spoke to him, because the shipment was already on its way to me.

Peter could not believe it and told me so. So I arranged for him to fly out to Kentucky and see the product. If it was there, which he thought impossible, he wanted to buy it. I told Peter when the shipment arrived.

"I'll be there tomorrow."

"Great."

Well tomorrow was the same day as this storm of storms.

Peter Weise arrived on schedule in New Jersey with a major problem for me… all of the flights to Kentucky had been canceled due to the storm.

"I'm going back home Adam." His thick German accent showed little emotion and his statement was more of an edict to me than a question.

"Wait. You've come this far. You have to see it for yourself."

"I have no way of getting to you."

My mind raced for a quick solution.

"If you give me 30 minutes I'll make sure you get here."

Peter thought of it. I imagine he wasn't thrilled about hopping right back on an airplane after a flight from Germany. At least I was hoping that was the case. He paused for what seemed like an eternity

"Okay. 30 minutes."

We hung up and all I could think was *helicopter.*

As someone who had hitched a ride on choppers throughout my military career, I knew that the flight from New York to me wasn't going to be very long. Problem was I had to find a company that would be willing to fly it in the snow.

Money talks, bullshit walks.

"I'll pay you double what it would normally cost. And you get to take him back."

The Helicopter company jumped at the opportunity.

Two hours later, I was shoveling snow in the middle of our lumber yard in Kentucky to give the chopper a place to land. I cleared a path for Peter to walk safely to the warehouse to see our supply.

As the chopper descended, the butterflies in my stomach were doing cartwheels. My nerves were shot.

"Welcome to Kentucky."

Peter nodded and said hello with a stoic look on his face. We were standing in a foot of snow and this guy was wearing sandals without socks and a windbreaker. I was freezing my ass off and this guy looked like he was headed to South Beach.

"Show me what you have."

I led Peter to the back of our warehouse. I could tell that our entire inventory impressed him. I'm sure he was thinking "This young guy in Kentucky has no clue what he's doing." As he stared at our piles of Lignum Vitae, a smile came across his face.

"Vow." This is the Best No Chicken Money I hat ever Seen In My Lyfe" He tried to make sure I didn't hear him, but I heard it loud and clear.

We spent the next hour talking business and sipping a beer. When he left, we had a deal and CBI was an international player in the lumber industry business.

Three weeks later I got a call from Stewart Sexton who worked for Nordisk. CBI's fate would soon be sealed.

Enter If You Like Leave If You Can

"Adam this is Stewart Sexton with Nordisk. How 'ya doing?"

The voice on the other end had a strong Southern accent that reminded me of one of my buddies from the Army. It was one part "Aw shucks" and one part instantly disarming.

Before I could answer, he continued.

"This is Stewart Sexton with Nordisk."

"Oh shit!" that was the first thought that came to mind.

Nordisk was the giant of the lumber industry. They did business with everyone and if you weren't doing business with them, then you were probably too insignificant to matter.

Nordisk was calling us because they wanted to do business with us!

Though there were many lumber companies around the world, it's really a tight knit industry where anyone can literally call anyone at any time. When we sold that 98,000 pounds of Lignum vitae, the ink hadn't dried on the deal before Nordisk and everyone else knew about it. We weren't supposed to be able to get that kind of product in that sort of abundance, so we went from playing in the minors to the big leagues.

A deal with Nordisk Timber represented another wrung on the ladder of success for CBI. But there was more to this deal than that. Cash flow was always a problem for our business. I had hoped that we would be able to work out a deal with Nordisk to help us with that.

From our initial call, Stewart and I began a weeks-long negotiation process to figure out how we could work together.

The major problem was that Nordisk wanted more wood than we could deliver to them because we didn't have the cash flow to pay for it all to be harvested. We relied on payment from companies once they had received their lumber, graded it and then gave the final "okay." This meant that at any given moment we would have more money out than coming in.

I trusted Stewart. We had good conversations, and he respected my business mind and approach. He asked me about the ins and outs of our business operations, mills we used, employees, work schedule, etc. He was amazed that we could do so much and we were so new to the industry. He liked that about us. We showed "guts" and tenacity. That was better than experience.

Eventually we struck the deal of a lifetime.

I made a deal with Nordisk lumber that allowed Nordisk's workers to place their lumber grader at the end of my sawmill and order their own trucks with their export seal and wire us money as soon as they graded the lumber!

There was no lag time for payment. No waiting for a check to arrive. It was almost instantaneous. This worked for Nordisk since the company would not have any risk regarding grade, volume, or ownership, and it worked out well for us because it essentially functioned as a blank check. When we knew we were getting money in, we could afford to cut more wood.

Our business grew dramatically. We went from one truck every two months, to two trucks a month, to one truck a week, and eventually to 40 trucks a week! We hired a third shift and worked around the clock. The Wood-Mizer mills used diesel engines, and the oil had to be changed every shift. This meant we needed more sawmills.

Instead, John decided we should buy more engines and swap out the motors each shift. It was less expensive and far more efficient time wise. Soon we had an engine oil change and repair shop and a blade sharpening room. John's idea was genius.

We had lights at night and the place looked like New York City. We blew transformers often because we were drawing so much from the grid. But it couldn't stop us.

We were felling trees like crazy. The Sound Surveillance System (SOSUS) must've been going crazy as massive trees tumbled to the ground in the Honduran jungle.

"Boom." The ground shook as each tree came crashing down. It was dangerous work and unfortunately several of our workers lost their lives. It was hard, manual labor.

Chainsaws were not allowed in the jungle. The Honduran government rightfully determined that removing the use of chainsaws would make cutting trees down much harder. So we had to use the two-handed saws to cut through these towering giants. It was exhilarating to watch as the culmination of all of the blood and sweat came tumbling down.

Still with all the noise from the falling timbers, I never really "heard" Nature's voice. I hadn't considered the environmental ramifications of what we were doing. I simply was naïve and unaware that any existed. I felt that we were doing a good thing for the people of Honduras. Sure, we were building a business but they were getting paid more than they could have ever imagined.

I felt good knowing that we were helping to improve their lives. Sometimes Dad would grab stacks of pizzas and just leave them out for the drivers and their families. The truckers loved us and why shouldn't they? We were honest and generous to everyone.

We had helped them changed their lives for the better for generations to come.

By 1994 we had so much cash flow going through Banco Atlantida that we became the 3rd largest business in Honduras.

Our operations were centralized in a region of Honduras known as Olancho. It was mountainous and rural with winding dirt roads and a village comprised of clusters of tiny shacks with dirt floors and thatched roofs. There was a sign on the side of the road that read "WELCOME TO OLANCHO. ENTER IF YOU LIKE, LEAVE IF YOU CAN." It wasn't anything like the city. The people didn't have much material wealth, but I always got the sense that they were happy.

Well, not everyone.

As Americans, we generally believe that most of our disputes with people in other countries tend to evolve from their general disdain for Americans and what we represent. We have freedoms that many in other countries simply don't have. We make choices on a daily basis about where we will go, what we will eat, how we will get there or whatever, that many around the world don't have an option to make those sorts of choices. Because of this, Americans have become accustomed to believing that the world simply hates us because we're American.

It wasn't that simple in Honduras, in fact, in most of Latin America. They didn't dislike Americans because of our freedom; they disliked us because of *money*.

More specifically because they felt like Americans had somehow taken all the money and therefore there wasn't any left for them to have. This ideology permeated every level of life in Latin America and Honduras, from the lowest economic levels to the government.

There was this sense that "since the Americans have all of the money, we need to get some of it, however we can." This meant that there were real cost to doing business and then there were those "hidden" cost much in the sense that the Italian Mob is known for "taxing" businesses, legal and otherwise, for the right to operate.

Locals would set up roadblocks to prevent our trucks from getting through and we'd have to pay a "fee" for their usage. Local Leaders charged us a fee to operate in their area. The government charged us for filing paperwork and then charged us again for submitting the paperwork. We didn't mind paying the locals. We understood what was going on. As far as the government was concerned, we hated it, but what could we do. It seemed like everyone was getting paid.

Well everyone wasn't getting paid.

Some of the Locals who had been left out of the money grab by their leaders started complaining about the traffic. This was directly a result of local politicians and some leaders stoking the fires of discontent to extort more money from us. We knew it too.

"Jimmy. Alex." I called the guys over one day after a visit from a man named Don who had told me that word was spreading about us being crooks in one of the local churches.

"What's up?" Jimmy was already ready for work.

"I need you to gather up 20 of our drivers and their families and go to church this Sunday."

"I don't go to church." Alex was serious, but so was I.

"This is for work."

It took a little convincing from Jimmy, but Alex knew he had to do it.

THE MAHOGANY MAFIA   41

Everyone in Honduras went to church on Sundays. It was the epicenter of many of the people's lives for social contact and relationships. It was also the best place to combat any bullshit that might be spreading about us.

Sunday came and we had several of our workers show up in their uniforms at the church with Jimmy and Alex. These were their friends and family members. People trusted their word and believed them. After church, our drivers and workers spoke with everyone during procession and afterward at coffee.

They shared wonderful stories about how great they were being treated and how great of a person Gringo Joe and "The Boss" were. We even had them say positive things about the official. It worked. No one wanted to be the one to say anything bad about a company full of church-going workers and law-abiding citizens. It was a masterful plan that we would later use several more times and it directly came from my work in Honduras with Colonel Les Thatcher, then the US Army Chief Intelligence Officer.

Olancho was an extremely dangerous place for anyone, but it was even worse for my Dad. He paid the truckers in cash and would keep these huge wads of money in the office. It wasn't a secret because he never tried to hide the money from anyone. Dad was like that. He had this air of invincibility about him. We both did.

One day as Dad was leaving the trail head where they load the trucks on the way to our mill, a man holding a pistol tried to rob him. Tito had gone to get the car and Dad was alone. Dad recognized the man but didn't know his name. Luckily one of the drivers had just pulled into the yard and he saw what was going on. He yelled to several other men, and they all came over. I had been on another side of the trail head about 30 yards away, so I hustled over to see what was happening.

The guy never stood a chance.

Everyone in Olancho carried guns, knives, and machetes. Dad was unbothered by the old thing.

"It was nothing." I looked as the man was dragged away screaming, I couldn't do anything for him, nor would I have tried.

That day the drivers and all the workers kept their yet-unstated pact. "If you fuck with Gringo Joe, then you fuck with all of us."

Gringo Joe was a made man from that moment forward. He was the open end of a wallet of cash paid faithfully to those who worked hard, delivered what was asked for, and closed it when the standards were not met.

Indeed, I realized something as I watched our guys leaving. Their loyalty to my Dad and Me had shit to do with their loving us as for some magical, familial reason.

It had everything to do with money.

As we drove away from Olancho and back to the city, my mind replayed the day's events. It could have ended so differently for my Dad, but he didn't give a shit. He was tossing back beers and laughing with Jimmy. I chugged a few myself and tried to relax. My mind was always racing about what to do next to build the business. I had kept reinvesting everything that we made, but I wasn't clear on how big we would grow to. "What should I do about the company in Japan? I need to call Peter Weiss. I have to finish the house. Did I miss anything?"

These and a million other things were what my twenty something year-old mind faced every night when I attempted to sleep. I closed my eyes for a bit and grabbed another beer. Dad had been talking about something Jimmy had said. I drifted back to earlier that day.

I knew that the more we kept going into Olancho, the greater our chances wee that we would not make it back home.

But I wasn't afraid.

Chapter 6.   Be Careful What You Ask For

"I want to go down to Honduras and see what it's like."

We were in the midst of our housewarming party and Catherine, and I were entertaining our friends in Elizabethtown, Kentucky.

The house was beautiful; perfect for us. It was a four-bedroom, three bathroom home and we believed that it would be the place we would retire to someday. It was just off the golf course and right on the corner of two streets that were lined with white picket fences and well mowed lawns. It was our idyllic life at the time.

Al and I had become great friends since that first meeting in Lowe's. Business-wise we had done a couple of small deals, but our friendship was much deeper than that. I was shocked to hear him say that he wanted to go to Honduras though.

"I want to go into the jungle and see the operation."

It's one thing to want to go to Honduras and be in La Ceiba. It's another world to go to Olancho.

"You're really nuts Al."

"I'm serious."

"And so am I. It's deep in the jungle Al. The only way to get from base camp to the jungle is on a wooden back board, on a mule."

"So…"

Al was determined.

"So… it's 10 hours one way."

Al didn't flinch. Inside I laughed. He had no idea what the he was about to sign up to do.

"What? You don't think I can't hack it?"

"Of course I do, but it's just… it's not easy."

I *knew* Al couldn't hack it. No one really *volunteered* to just go gallivanting into the jungle on the back of a mule for 10 hours.

This was a two-way trip!

Al was in his early to mid 50's at the time. He wasn't about to let a twenty-something year old out do him. He was determined and who was I to stop him.

A few weeks later, Al landed in Honduras, ready for his jungle adventure. We spent some time in La Ceiba and then I toured him around our receiving warehouse. He was shocked at the extent of our operation and in my mind this all only legitimized our business in his eyes.

"What about the mules?"

"Oh it's coming," I told him.

Me, Al, and Jimmy hitched a ride with one of our trucks headed to the ranch to pick up wood. It was a 3-hour ride in the back of a flatbed truck with bad shocks and a driver who didn't give a shit.

The sun was barely coming up as we ascended into the mountains. The cool jungle air soon overtook the humidity-laden temperatures of the coastal region. Jimmy laughed heartily as he told stories about what had been going on at the mill recently. The clean, crisp air seemed to invigorate him, if that was at all possible.

Jimmy and I had traveled this route many times before and I had become accustomed to the thin air at the higher elevations. I could tell Al was trying to adjust his breathing and gave him shit for not "being in shape." Jimmy's high-pitched laugh could be heard for miles down in the valleys below.

Three hours later we arrived at the Ranch which was our drop-off point for our lumber. Several trucks were already ahead of us and were being loaded with wood. The mules would bring the lumber down from the jungle and then the trucks would pick it up and take it down to our mills where John and the guys would then get it loaded for shipment. It was a laborious process, but no one seemed to care. I think we all felt good knowing that we were putting in a "good day's work," everyday.

It was freezing at this point. It was nothing for the temperatures to get down in the low 40's up high in the Switchback Mountains and Al was freezing and worn out. 10 hours later we arrived at the logger's base camp, still 2 hours from where the tree cutting was happening.

THE MAHOGANY MAFIA 45

There was this long rectangle-shaped shed on the premises about 70 feet long 30 feet wide. It had a thatched palm roof. Inside of it was a long mud stove and two ladies who were going to cook for the loggers and us.

"I'm sleeping here! It's going to be warm." Al was emphatic and loud with his declaration.

"No Amigo." One of our Honduran workers interjected.

"Es No Bueno."

"Why not?" Al thought the guy was trying to claim the space for himself. He hadn't been to Honduras before, and I think there was a cultural misunderstanding. Al seemed to think the guy was trying to tell him he couldn't sleep where he wanted, and Al had decided he was going to *"sleep wherever he wanted."* Al eventually won out and the guy shrugged his shoulders and looked at me and Jimmy. We shrugged too, though Jimmy flashed a devilish-smirk at me.

There was a loft space in there where they kept all the feed for the mules. They put all the feed up above in the loft and under that, that's where Al determined he was going to lay his head.

The rest of us slept in thatched-roof huts on the ground, wrapped in blankets and layers of clothing to keep us warm.

The next morning, I heard, Al scream before I actually saw him. He sounded like someone was cutting his nuts off or something with a dull blade. I ran to the shed with Jimmy and the others in tow. When we got there it was bad. Real bad.

Al was covered from head to toe with these giant, jungle ticks. They were like dogs, they were so damn big. They were everywhere

Jimmy burst out laughing and the Hondurans tried to hide their faces.

"I need to go to the fucking ER!" Al was in tears and desperately removing ticks from his arms and legs.

"There is no ER Al. We are in the middle of the jungle!" I went over to try and help him. He pulled down his underwear and ticks were everywhere. He was pulling them from his scrotum, 2 at a time. The ones he couldn't reach, on the places they shouldn't have been, I had to help him. He was miserable, and everyone was laughing their asses off.

And we hadn't even been to the tree cutting and worse, we had still had the 10 hour mule ride back to the logging drop off point.

"My fucking ass is raw!" Al bellowed in misery as we traversed the mountain terrain on our journey.

Of course, it was. The only way to ride on the back of the mules was to sit across a piece of un-sanded wood that had been thrown across the back of one of the mules. The road rash is painful and real. I could feel my own underwear sticking to my legs as my skin chaffed and eventually rubbed raw.

All I could think about was the ride coming back.

You can't get off and walk, because there are snakes every where and nearly all of them are poisonous. You're at the mercy of the jungle and sometimes this can be unnerving.

The ride to the location of a tree cutting, through the Switchback Mountains did possess a certain beauty and serenity to it. Other than our talking and laughter (at Al's expense) the lush green vegetation and growth covered by the canopy of trees, couldn't help but make you give pause and consider your life.

"My ass hurts."

Al's bellyaching always snapped me back to reality.

We heard the trees falling long before we arrived at the tree cutting area. I was always in awe at the sheer size of those gigantic Mahogany trees. It was truly something to behold.

We loaded up the wood on the mules and got ready for the two-hour ride back down to base camp. Al groaned with anticipation at the prospect of having to do this again. Jimmy was eating this shit up.

"He told you not to sleep there."

"Fuck you, Jimmy."

Jimmy laughed it off. He knew Al was frustrated and hurting but in the jungle that didn't mean shit.

Once we were done, we began our trek back down the mountain. Al couldn't get comfortable on his mule to save his life. Jimmy was meanwhile performing his duties as General Manager; making sure we kept moving at the right pace, keeping us together and safe, all of that stuff.

And serving as Al's personal GPS update.

"How much longer do we have?"

"It's just around the bend a bit."

For 10 hours that's all we heard. Al was in real pain. The Hondurans laughed their asses off every time Al asked Jimmy "How much further?'

Finally, after a few hours, Al asked again.

"How much further?"

All of the Hondurans responded in unison.

"Just around the bend."

They cracked themselves up. Jimmy belted out his hearty laughs and Al cursed everyone out. He wasn't really angry, just in pain, but he played his part in the joke.

That was the first and last time that Al came to Honduras. Our friendship grew even closer after that trip, but how could it not when you have to help a guy pick ticks off of his balls.

There was a strong camaraderie that was built among the guys that traveled up into the jungle on those mules. It reminded me of my military days when your unit was your family. Unfortunately, my Dad could never experience this. He weighed 340 pounds at the time, and he simply was too big. He didn't mind it seemed, but I wondered if it was just a cover up. For a guy that was always the life of the party, this was one party he could never attend.

Because of his weight, Dad developed Sleep Apnea, which was further complicated by his lifestyle of eating everything and drinking and smoking as much as he liked. Treatment options weren't very reliable in Honduras, so we started flying him up to Florida to go to a Sleep Apnea clinic there. I would fly with him back to the states to get treatments and then we'd either go back to Honduras together or I'd fly home for a few days to see Catherine.

One day as we were traveling, he said something to me that stuck with me.

"All I want is a boat. Here. Maybe somewhere close to you and Catherine. I could live there."

I had never really heard him talk about a boat before, let alone about living near Catherine and me. It shocked me, but it stuck with me for some reason.

Back in Honduras, business was steady, and everyone wanted what we were selling. I had to hire 2 new accountants to help with payroll and balancing our books. Meanwhile, I was negotiating with Theodore Nagle again and with Yau Leun Timber in Hong Kong. We had put together some brochures and marketing materials and shipped them all over the world. We included testimonials and referrals from all of our past customers and once buyers found out we could deliver the goods, they wanted in on the action.

Cocoa Bola, Lignum Vitae, Rosewood, Mahogany, you name it we had it. It seemed like every time the guys cut down a tree in the jungle it was some exotic species that the world hadn't seen in half a century.

Hogue Grips, a high-end manufacturer of hand grips for guns wanted to use our wood for their inventory. Rolls Royce wanted our Mahogany for the interior of their luxury line of vehicles. Someone in Australia wanted our wood for musical instruments. We were sending wood everywhere, but we were also spending money like crazy too.

Dad sent me a note when I was back in Kentucky. He needed shotgun shells for 10 and 12 gauge shot guns, a million candle watt light, a new bobcat forklift with a 4 foot bucket , 2 refrigerators, 3 freezers, clothes washers and dryers, 4 stove tops, 3 motorbikes, a water pump, Van taillight with paint, 50 pounds of Food, parrot seeds, blue plastic tarps, rat traps, 2 chainsaws (at the mill), 2 shotguns, guitar straps. anchor seal compressor, and a spray gun in the new Bronco truck, which I had no idea what the hell that was.

It was like we were running our own music shop, laundromat, and gun range on the company dime. I bitched and moaned about it, but he assured me he needed everything so I got everything. I had to take care of Jimmy with some back pay (he had deferred payments) and ultimately we settled on a deal that made him a 3% owner of CBI stock.

Jimmy had always wanted to own a business and he deserved to be a part of the ownership team.

I had to get back to Honduras. Before I left, I wrote a letter to Theodor Nagle because Peter hadn't bought our Lignum. This was going to put us in a pinch financially and it wasn't going to be good. There was so much going on, all at once, that all I wanted to do was get back to Honduras, do a quick assessment, leave, and sell some more wood to keep us afloat.

When I arrived I hurried to our lumber yard. Most of the drivers were in the yard and waiting for Dad to pay them. I went to my office and sat down. Soon there was a knock on the door. It was Luis, Dad's bodyguard.

"What's up Boss. We've got a problem."

"What's going on?" I got up, gathered my shit, and put my pistol on my hip.

"There's some guys here looking for money. And they've got big guns."

Chapter 7. Corruption And Betrayal

When I walked into the yard, I didn't know what to expect. How many men were there? What kind of weaponry did they have? Why are they looking for money? I nodded to Luis, and he knew my mind immediately: go and gather up the guys and close the gate. There was only one way in and one way out of our U.S. Sponsored Free Trade Zone lumber yard. If these guys wanted a problem, they were about to get everything they needed.

When I rounded the bend, I was confronted by three heavily armed men. I instantly knew that they weren't our guys. I did recognize the truck they were driving as one of our logger's from Olanchito, and I immediately spotted blood on the side of the truck. Luis came back, walking painfully slow with our whole yard (about 30 armed workers) in tow. Dad was among them.

The Men looked at me. The leader, a short guy with a thin mustache who wasn't wearing a shirt stepped forward. Dumb ass. All of our workers wore uniforms. Even the drivers. If you weren't wearing a uniform, you weren't related to us and you certainly were no driver. It was an honest way to keep the police and robbers off of your back, because everyone knew who and where we were. We had paid them all off to give us safe passage through the mountains and the uniforms defined that safe passage.

I nodded and Luis began to speak.

"What would you like?"

"We want to get paid for our wood."

I sized him up. Did this guy think that we were stupid. I surveyed the guys around me. The gate was locked and our men were armed. At best, I figured these three guys could've shot two of us before they were killed. I wasn't sure about what they had waiting on the outside of the fence though.

I had a quick decision to make. This was about to turn ugly. Our workers were pissed, and I could feel them itching to pull their guns on these guys. A shootout would've been disastrous for us. We were an international company doing business in a foreign country under an agreement to strengthen the economy of the host nation. CBI would've made international headlines and my picture would've been broadcasted on every channel around the globe. I quickly played this entire scenario through my mind, and I reacted like the officer I had been trained to be.

"Okay. Tell him that we will take a look at what he has and if we like it we will buy it."

Luis's look was incredulous. *"Are we really going to do business with these guys?"*

"And make sure to tell them they have to turn over their weapons first."

Luis translated my message and the lead guy looked at his partners and mouthed something to them. All three nodded in agreement and they dropped their weapons to the ground. Two of our guys swooped in and picked them up.

Now we were completely in control. I had already determined that they weren't carrying any other guns and if they were, it would've been in their socks, which would've taken too long to get to. I had my guys go and offload the lumber while I walked the guys over to where Dad was back in his office. Several of the workers walked with us.

I turned to Luis, "Tell them we are going to pay them for their work…"

Luis obliged as we walked into the office and sure enough we handed the men their money.

Then I turned to the short leader and spoke directly to him, and I looked into his eyes as we walked out.

"That truck belongs to us. We are keeping it. If you ever come back here again, we will have you arrested. Or worse. Do not step foot inside this gate again in your life."

He looked me squarely in the eyes and nodded as if understanding. Luis realized there was no need to improve my Spanish.

I escorted them to the gate and the guys let them out, but not before everyone had gotten a good look at who these men were. Once the gate was opened, they quickly took off. Disappearing down the road.

That was the last that anyone ever saw of them.

That day didn't slow us down. We went right back to business as usual: Dad still walked around with bundles of cash in his briefcase with Luis on his side. Jimmy still was Jimmy, John kept the Mill functioning and I kept paying everyone who taxed us for doing business.

That shit irritated me. I had always tried to do right by our workers and even by the sharks who wanted to charge us for government paperwork, or even the police who we had to pay for "protection." But it seemed like the more we gave, the more they would ask; especially the government officials.

I had already known many in the Honduran government were corrupt. I knew how they maneuvered and operated and so I made it a point to make sure that I always had every permit and piece of paperwork necessary to ensure that our shipments would leave Honduras intact and with little resistance. And I wrote everything down in my green journal. Every single transaction and encounter. Every meeting, every outcome, every person. I wrote down what I thought about that morning and needed to do by the end of the day. It was that hyper-vigilance that allowed me to know who was shaking me down.

The guy at the Customs office would charge me $200 for a piece of paper that should've cost $20. I almost told him to "fuck off" at least 100 times, but I bit my tongue. Still, it was starting to get to me.

For a cash strapped company those sorts of things added up. Sure, we were surviving, but things seemed to be closing in.

One day John came to me with some information.

"Holy Week is coming up."

I might've been named Adam and my sister Eve and my brother Joseph, but we weren't religious people. Holy Week was like every other week in our house. We may have gone to church once or twice, but I wasn't an observer.

"Okay."

That's all I could really respond with.

"The workers won't work during Holy Week."

"What!"

That shit almost made me blow a gasket. We had customers who were anticipating shipments. If we didn't get their lumber to them on time, our good reputation that we had worked so hard to achieve, would be shot.

"They have to work. We can't afford to shut down."

"No, you don't understand. This is a very important time for them. No one works, no matter what."

John's solemn look made me realize that there was no wiggle room on this.

But there had to be.

Most of our workers were Catholic. Many drove with silver, medallion-encrusted Crosses hanging from the mirrors in their trucks. They all prayed before they ate a meal, and everyone attended church on Sundays. I didn't know what to do.

I had finally squared things up with Nordisk and Jimmy's cousin Eminillo was in Catacamas trying to expand our business ventures there, so this couldn't have come at a worse time.

Dad and I tried to put our heads together to work out something.

"If we take off a whole week this will kill us."

"If we make them work they simply won't show up. And they will resent us for not being empathetic to their religious beliefs."

I knew Dad was right, but I also realized that he didn't understand the bigger picture of our business.

"Andy by the way, I think we need a new Bobcat."

What?

We had just bought a brand new Bobcat and now we needed another one. Dad was eating through our money like a tapeworm through cheese. But it wasn't his fault. The terrain was rough and the wear and tear on the vehicles was undeniable, but still it just seemed like everyone had their hand out.

The stress of it all began to affect my health. My PTSD was getting worse, and my physical health was affected as well. I felt sick, tired, even defeated at one point. *"I couldn't let it end like this."*

We couldn't shut down operations, that simply wasn't an option. CBI wasn't even a year old; we hadn't built up enough relationship equity. A few days later I met with some of the leaders of the workers, and we started talking about what it would take to keep working during Holy Week.

They pushed back as I expected they would. I eventually had to ask them what it would take, even though I already knew the answer.

"Money."

Doing business in Honduras had already taught me so much about money and what it does to people. For a sheltered kid from New York who had never really had much money (even in the military, soldiers don't deal with money), it was an eye-opening experience. People were willing to risk their lives for money and certainly would kill for it. There were no limitations on what money would make someone do.

In the end, I had to pay our workers double their normal pay for them to work during Holy Week and I also made modifications for those who wanted to attend church services. We continued rolling past Good Friday and Easter.

When I finally made it back home there was barely any time to stop and take a breath. It seemed there was always a missing bill of lading or an issue with a shipment. We used Seaboard for our international shipments and often between Honduras and Miami something would go wrong. Then from Miami we would go to the Port of Charleston, and something would go wrong there. Then from the Port of Charleston everything would be put on a train and taken to Manning, South Carolina. We were efficient and quick, but the growing pains of a business did not escape us.

So that was my day, constantly faxing and making calls to customers and searching for Bills of lading. Mike Reiber, my old Army buddy who I had hired when we first started the business, was doing a great job for us domestically with our sales and he kept us busy. In between faxes and phone calls, I also worked the lines for international sales.

One day I got a call from Kagiya Lumber and Hokoshu Lumber in Japan. They wanted some of our lumber. The Japanese customers preferred to do business in person, so Catherine and I hopped a flight and went to Japan.

Absolutely beautiful country! We enjoyed the cuisine and closed the deal. While there we decided to make a stop in Hong Kong as well.

When we returned Mike Reiber called to let me know that Muhammad Aziz wanted 300,000 board feet a year. Aziz operated a small operation in the States and he wanted in on the action.

I spoke to Wendy again at Yao Leun in Hong Kong.. They were interested in our Lignum Vitae and Mahogany, and they wanted to come out to Kentucky to see us and our inventory. Yao Leun was an extremely successful family-owned business that had been in existence for years. They loved the sturdiness of the Honduran Mahogany and Lignum Vitae.

THE MAHOGANY MAFIA   55

At that time, given the Brazilian moratorium on the export of Swietenia Macrophylla, (Mahogany) CBI was the only company in the world that had the permit to export these species of lumber anywhere in the world. Customers literally had to come to us and we had to deliver.

And that's what they did. Wendy and her team flew from Hong Kong to Kentucky and met us. Catherine and I hosted them for dinner, and they saw our inventory firsthand. I guess it was still hard for people to believe that we actually had everything that we claimed in our fliers and brochures. I always smiled inside when I saw the look on their faces when they left.

They left without us having a deal.

A few weeks later, I got a call from Wendy and she and her family invited us back to Hong Kong to stay with them! Catherine and I were beside ourselves. We were still young. We weren't seasoned world travelers yet and these kinds of things didn't seem to happen for people like us, but they were.

We flew to Hong Kong and went to Wendy's place. It was opulent and majestic with the finest hand-carved wooden statues and furniture I had ever seen. It was as if we were in a palace.

We were treated with the best hospitality and kindness that I had experienced. Wendy appreciated what we did for them when they came to the states. This was her way of showing their gratitude.

After dinner, they asked me to give them my quotes again.

I had prepared my numbers and presentation and gladly went through each line item, detail by detail to explain how I arrived at my price, which was $25/square foot. When I finished, they all simply looked at me. I wasn't sure if had said something wrong or if our price was in fact too high.

Wendy and her team began to talk in her native Chinese. Catherine and I didn't understand a word of it, but she looked at me, smiled brightly and said,

"You need to triple your price right now."

I leaned in to make sure I heard her correctly.

"Say what?"

"You need to triple your price right now. Whatever you have to say, go back, and say you made a mistake and give them a new quote."

I looked around the room. I trusted Catherine. I stood up.

"Everyone. Everyone. I am so sorry. I made a mistake. I made a misquote."

They all looked at me. Catherine's eyes darted from me to Wendy to the rest of her group. And then back to me.

"I left out one of the most important line items and I am so sorry I made a math error, It's not $25 a square foot, it's $75 a square foot."

I let my new price hang in the air and for eternity it just sat there without a response. Then Wendy smiled and said a few more words to her team.

Finally, she turned to me and said,

"Okay. We'll take it."

Just like that. Without even batting an eye.!

Meanwhile, Stewart Sexton and I spoke nearly every day. We were constantly confirming shipments and money wires His brother John at Hickory Lumber in North Carolina had also become one of Stewart's customers, so that only added to the relationship. Stewart was always cordial and welcoming, often times pointing me in the right direction for more business. Nordisk was our biggest customer and really without them we would've never been able to stay afloat. As quick as Nordisk and Stewart would wire money, I would send it down to my Dad in Honduras to pay our guys; $22,000 on May 18th; $10,000 on May 27; $10,000 on June 3rd, the money outflow was endless.

One day I got a call from a guy who owned a company called Caoba De Honduras. Caoba was "Mahogany" in Spanish. He wanted to do business with us. He was particularly interested in what is known as Green Common Mahogany at 8/4 (wood is only labeled or sold in quarters. So instead of saying 2 inches, you would say 8/4). He offered me a price that was nearly 50% less than what I normally got for our wood.

"I don't have the resources that you have, and I am trying to keep my prices down."

My initial reaction was to tell him to "go get the timber from the jungle yourself," but I had matured in my thinking.

Perhaps I was still remembering the Holy Week incident and I wanted to make sure that I did the right thing. We talked a bit more and I liked the guy. I agreed to meet him for dinner in La Ceiba.

His name was Michael Canahuati.

THE MAHOGANY MAFIA

Death And Money In The Jungle

"I want to keep the manufacturing jobs in Honduras."

That was Canahuati's primary pitch to me. I understood his plight and I wanted to help him do this. I figured there was enough lumber to go around for all of us.

I was naïve as hell.

As we sipped wine and talked, I quickly formed an opinion about the guy; he seemed okay. I didn't think too much more about doing business with him.

By this time in our business development, we were paying our employees weekly payroll. Nordisk had asked for all of the lumber we could provide in all grades of quality. Nordisk also would pay for some upfront of our lumber and have it shipped to them.

This allowed us to give them a better price. This us course allowed Nordisk to buy at a lower price from us and earn a margin. It was a shrewd business deal on his part and it also helped us because we had higher revenues and better cash flows than we otherwise would have.

By 1994, the supply of lumber from the jungle for us seemed endlessly available. While we were big movers and shakers, we still were not able to buy everything that could be cut. Our workers knew that due to cash flow constraints, if they wanted to make more money, they couldn't do it with us.

So began a black market, a bunch of side-hustles, which increased supply. It wasn't illegal and we knew that it existed. Our workers would cut down more than we could buy and find places to sell it. Canahuati undoubtedly benefited from this too because he could buy lumber there also. The only thing was that the 'extra' side hustle volume was limited, because we bought the majority of the lumber and always could buy the best quality.

CBI's infrastructure helped create this entire ancillary market. While we didn't receive a dime from it, I knew that it was free enterprise, and it didn't bother me. I was busily trying to make sure we met all our orders and paid the people we needed to keep business flowing.

The more that we grew the more this extra lumber grew. The guys in the jungle who were doing the cutting had an entrepreneurial spirit, so they figured "we'll just keep cutting." As this continued Caoba de Honduras' warehouse holdings of lumber improved.

Canahuati's business was primarily in the furniture parts business. As he bought our excess lumber, he would get increasingly different widths and cuts of lumber. This meant he would have an improved ability to sell more furniture parts to different places. He needed CBI to thrive, so his business could thrive.

This was a good relationship for Canahuati, and we garnered all sorts of international acclaim for the wood we were pulling out of the jungle.

Dad kept his manual with him to identify wood species, and we sent faxes and detailed photographs to experts everywhere in case we discovered something we didn't easily recognize.

We were featured on the cover of <u>Fine Woodworking</u> Magazine and <u>Fine Furniture Daily.</u> CBI's name became synonymous with fine products and more and more people wanted to do business with us.

Yao Leun ended up placing 4 orders with us for Lignum Vitae. They were stockpiling it at the tune of 80,000 plus pounds a shipment. I admired their foresight. They were looking to become the only provider of the lumber as it became more and more scare. It was a great business position, and I had no qualms with it.

Business was in high gear and it looked like nothing was going to stop us. Still, we weren't immune from the perils of lumbering.

That summer, we had several shipments of Coco Bolo that needed to go out to our customers in the States. The trucks had all come in, but our numbers didn't add up. Dad, Jimmy and John generally kept a great inventory of what came and left our lumber yard. Dad and I had had many arguments about the need to be precise about how much lumber we shipped and where it went. He didn't always see things this way, but some strategic "nurturing" on my part had helped him understand that if we made a mistake in our paperwork, it could cost us everything.

"We're missing a truck load of lumber."

John scoured the yard in search of the wood. Jimmy checked his manifest and soon we realized that there was indeed a truck that was missing.

This wasn't a case of selling excess. This was wood that had been accounted for and we expected to have in our yard. Had they stolen it from us? No one stole from CBI; especially people we had worked with. John found out that the missing shipment was with one of our trucks that was operated by a family. I had seen them several times in the yard in the past. It was the Mom and Dad and their two young kids.

We waited a few more hours for the truck, but nothing. As we began to prepare to send another truck out to go and get another load from the jungle, two of our guys came running up to me.

"They're gone Boss."

"What do you mean?"

I could tell by the distressed look on their faces that something bad had happened. My first thought was that they were killed by robbers and the truck was stolen. We had already been through that before. No one could've been dumb enough to do that again.

But that wasn't it.

"They drowned." I felt a sharp pain in my gut. We had lost workers before, especially in the jungle, but this kind of hit home. Catherine and I had been talking about starting our own family soon and this sparked some sort of change within myself. I had thought about what it would be like to be a father and how hard I would work to not make the same mistakes that my own father had made.

We all listened as the guys explained what happened.

The family was on their way back to the warehouse with their lumber and accidentally drove off one of the steep embankments by the river that flowed from the mountains. This wasn't unusual because erosion along the cliffs near the river was a constant in Honduras.

At any given moment, between the rain and the river flooding some of these roads could have steep drop-offs, and getting out was nearly impossible. This is what happened to them.

They drove off of the road and one of Honduras's infamous flash floods occurred, causing the river to swell so rapidly and with such fast moving currents they all were swept away and drowned. It was a sobering moment. The pursuit of a better life for themselves had cost these people their lives.

There was a long pause between us all.

"We'll go and get the lumber."

Another driver stepped forward. He recognized that we had to fill the shipment. I don't think he was affected by this family dying or maybe he knew that there was nothing else that we could do. As a soldier I was prepared to die and have others around me die in battle. This wasn't a battlefield though.

I nodded to the guy and he and his crew set out for the three-hour drive-up to the ranch.

"I need to tell you something." Dad had a serious look on his face, and I wasn't sure what was eating at him. We walked over to the office and sat down underneath the light of a dull lamp. Jimmy laughed loudly outside. Things quickly turned back to normal.

"We're getting big Adam. They're going to come for us."

"Who?"

Dad leaned forward in his chair as if trying to keep someone from hearing him.

"I don't know. It's Honduras."

"You're worrying about nothing. We're good."

I didn't really have time for this kind of talk from my Dad. But it seemed like there was more that he wanted to say.

"Whatever happens, don't you ever let those mutherfuckers take what we've built. OK?"

"No one's taking anything from us. Okay."

A few weeks later, I was in the office faxing some paperwork to Nordisk and I heard a commotion out in the yard. Jimmy peeked his head in the door.

"Somebody's here to see you."

I couldn't tell if Jimmy knew the person or not, but he didn't look too worried. Of course, Jimmy never looked worried. He had no reason to be. His pistol was loaded and on his hip at all times.

I got up and went outside and there was one of our guys. He had what must've been 50 truckers standing behind him. He smiled as I approached.

"Hey Boss. How's it going?"

I recognized the guy for sure though I couldn't think of his name at that exact moment. He was one of the truckers who would haul wood from the jungle for us and sometimes he would make deliveries down at the Port. He was an honorable guy and I liked him.

"I'm good. What's going on?"

"I need to borrow $200,000."

He didn't crack a smile and I knew he wasn't joking.

He had a look on his face that told me he was in some sort of dire straits.

"Do you have a shipment? If so I'll buy it?"

"No. I don't."

Again, there was no smile. Just an intense look of someone who had decided that this was his best option. *What the hell would he need $200 grand for in Honduras?"*

I couldn't come up with any sort of reason for this. Whatever it was, it was bigger than me. But this was how business operated. I was used to having money extorted from me by those government scumbags all of the time. Everyone knew or at least thought that we had money so our inherent and implied costs of doing business had gone up significantly.

But this was different. He was here in front of me with his team of drivers. Like any business owner, which I believed he was, since he had corralled all the drivers to begin with, there were going to be tough times. I could surely empathize with this.

"Okay. Let me see what I can do."

I grabbed my Dad from the grill where he had been slow roasting a pig. The enticing aroma of a slow cooked hog filled the steamy, jungle air. Today was going to be a great day for all the workers who happened to be around later in the evening.

"He wants what!"

I had to laugh at the irony in this. Dad had always been the one who overpaid our workers and tipped everyone extra. I bitched about it all the time. Now I wanted to help someone and the roles had reversed.

"Yeah. He's good for it."

Dad wanted to help the guy too. That's just who he was. But he had been feeling a bit of paranoia lately and I think he was just trying to make sure we didn't get caught pissing in the wind.

We walked over to the office together and went to the safe.

I called the guy into the office by himself and he watched as Dad counted out $200,000 cash in front of him. We put the money in a bag and handed it to the guy.

"Thank you Boss."

He nodded to both of us and was quickly on his way.

"He's good for it." Dad smiled at me as we locked up the safe.

He was good for it. He brought those truckers with him as a sort of "collateral" for me to see that he had people who worked for him.

Whatever deal he had worked out with those guys was between them. He just wanted to show us that he had the means to pay us back.

From that day on, I never paid that guy again until he and his men worked off every penny of that money.

I'm sure word got out that Gringo Joe and The Boss had given the guy this money, but we weren't worried, at least I wasn't. We were in the middle of the jungle and fear wasn't an emotion we chose to operate with.

Michael Canahuati and I had started to spend more time talking on the phone and even meeting up when he would drive up to La Ceiba. I liked his ambition and his vision. We laughed and joked often over Scotch or Tequila. He was grateful for the business that we allowed him to have.

"Stewart Sexton is a really good guy."

"Who'd you say?"

I wasn't sure I had heard him correctly. I didn't know that he knew Stewart.

"Stewart Sexton. I know him. Well kind of. I know his brother John a little bit better."

"Okay."

We continued with our conversation, but that night I went home and made a note in my ledger about Canahuati's comment. This struck me as strange, though I didn't think there was anything nefarious going on.

Our most dangerous enemy wasn't going to come out of the jungle.

Chapter 8. Resolute Decisions

"What'd they say?"

"I gotta take some pills."

Dad showed me a bottle but didn't bother to explain much more.

That was it. No real explanation after that. I knew better than to ask anymore so we went back to business as usual.

His lifestyle didn't change, so I figured he was going to be okay.

Dad had become incredibly adept at distinguishing lumber species and grades. Nordisk had two of their graders on site to ensure the wood quality and our overall process flowed like water through an iron pipe. We were seamless and efficient.

The local mayors and bankers loved us. They would have these big ass grins on their faces when they saw us coming. The bankers knew we would utilize their bank services. The mayors and other elected officials knew that we would pay our business "fees" promptly. We were pumping money into the local economies of several small towns and cities and with Canahuati and Caoba de Honduras doing business off of us further south, we were helping Hondurans all over the country.

Still, I knew that most of them hated us.

They had a belief that as Americans we were there to take something from them. It was that inherent distrust that existed coupled with a real need to do business with us because there wasn't any other business.

They *had* to work with us.

The VP of Honduras wrote a letter to me thanking me for coming to Honduras and doing business there, all the while feeling that resentment of Americans. As happy as they were that we were doing business there, I had no doubts that if given the opportunity there would be people in the cities who would've gladly done what they could to get us the hell out of Honduras.

We were folk heroes in the country though. Those people genuinely loved us, but of course, that was because we were the money source.

This realization only pushed me harder as I worked to continue to build CBI. It made me want to push harder to ensure that our business continued to grow and that we wouldn't fail. That was our motivation.

I worked like the proverbial fire stoker who poked the fire with one hand and then added fuel to the flame with the other. For me, it was the balancing act of drumming up more international business and massaging those relationships while also reaching out to U.S.-based companies. I wasn't supplying those companies; that territory belonged to Nordisk, but I had to reach out to them, nonetheless.

Our relationship with Nordisk was thriving, but they were such a big part of our overall business, I knew that I needed to protect our interests. If they somehow were to go out of business or if our relationship went sour at any point, we would be screwed. We had more of a gentlemen's agreement and there wasn't any sort of exclusivity clause between us, but I didn't want to piss them off. I also wasn't trying to shit in their bed.

I called Lane Stanton Vance, Craig Lumber; Wayne Stanton and every other American heavy hitters there were. I wanted them to know, I knew everyone. I was a loyalist and I made sure they all understood that and knew that my call was merely an introduction.

Sort of.

I also knew that this put Nordisk on notice too. This was a subtle way of letting them know that if they screwed with me in some way, I had options. I knew where to find the money and the customers. I gave myself an even space at the table, which in turn gave me some market vertical security.

Even with Nordisk backing us, that only allowed us to be paid "per-order" from them. We always needed money for our international orders and thus cash flow was once again an issue. For this reason, I had to meet with bankers regularly to secure loans for reinvestment in our company for equipment and other needs. Though we had always been good with our loans, questions arose. One day I was with one of our bankers and Nordisk came up.

"You have a major concentration of account risk with your Nordisk deal."

"I know."

"Well… what are you doing about it?" I could tell he had a bit of skepticism about the whole thing.

"You may think that I have only 1 customer, but the truth is I have a commodity. It has a value and as such it will always be needed. I could die tomorrow, and the stuff would sell."

I let those words hang in the air for a moment. He puffed hard on the cigarette he was holding and blew the smoke out. I knew he understood what I tried to tell him.

"And besides, I've called and introduced myself to all their U.S. customers. We're covered."

He would've given me a million dollars that day in denominations of $10 bills had I asked. I'm glad that I didn't.

With me making international and domestic calls daily, word of our relationship with Nordisk spread like wildfire.

In the jungle, as in war, every decision felt like a chess move with lives in the balance. I carried a green notebook just like in the military, jotting down every risk, every variable, every contingency. Preparation wasn't just a habit; it was a shield. Soldiers—and now my business partners—counted on it. Worrying about the details in advance meant fewer surprises when it mattered most.

I talked to Stewart Sexton every day. He always had questions about our inventory and wanted to know how things were going. I gladly answered and we'd spend time on the phone discussing new ideas and ways to grow what was already a bustling business.

CBI had only started less than a year earlier. We were already a major player in the lumber business. No one had done what we were currently doing.

"It was about 50 years ago."

Dad and I were tying up some things in the office and he had a pensive look. He was in the midst of telling me something about another foreign company that had been in the wood business in Honduras. Jimmy was seated in his chair, slowly rocking back and forth, the way he always did.

"Is this another story?"

Jimmy laughed.

Luis grinned and brushed his hair back. Dad grinned too.

"I'm just telling you the facts."

Dad wasn't one to get offended easily; either by choice or his sheer lack of picking up on the social cues around him.

"Alright so what happened?"

I knew he was going to finish telling the story whether we listened or not, so I figured it was just best to let him run with it.

"They nationalized the company. Threw some of them in prison. And killed some of them."

Luis smirked.

"Nobody's killing anybody these days."

"Maybe not, but they've done it before."

None of us were concerned, but Dad felt like it was something to know.

"These fuckers have been trying to extort more money from us every time we walk into that fucking office."

I knew he was right because I was the one having to pay $200 bucks for a $20 form three times a week.

"That was a Mexican company."

I knew there was no way anyone would try and take over our company. We were Americans. Like Made Men in La Cosa Nostra. To touch us, the United States government would have to get involved. Mitch McConnell was my Senator from Kentucky. He was one of the most powerful leaders in the Senate. We were super protected.

"That's not going to happen to us."

We all shared a laugh in agreement and that was the end of it.

Canahuati and Caoba De Honduras continued to request small orders from us. It was usually eh realm of 7,500-10,000 board feet of our 2 Common Green Mahogany (which was best for his furniture needs) at 8/4 thickness. This was nothing for us, but a substantial amount of business for him. With so much success in such a short period of time for us, smaller lumber operations began to pop up. They posed no threat to us at all, as they didn't have the bandwidth and infrastructure to compete with us, and frankly we welcomed their entrance into the industry. After all, they needed to buy most of their lumber from us as well.

That year Catherine and I had planned to have a big bash at our house on the 4th of July. It wasn't going to be anything extravagant, but just a good time with our neighbors and friends. Most of our neighbors weren't sure of exactly what our business was. They knew that I was some sort of "lumberman" and we had built our home from scratch, seemingly coming out of nowhere. We were probably 20 years younger than most of the couples that we were around, but they were our friends anyway.

I had a new deck built out of some of our Mahogany from the warehouse and it was beautiful. Everyone marveled at it and the hardwood floors we had in our place. I explained that this was from the jungles of Honduras and told stories about my adventures there in between flipping burgers and steaks. But I couldn't totally enjoy myself. There was too much shit on my mind.

I needed to get John trained at the National Hardwood Lumber Association, which wasn't a big deal, but it just added to the cluster of things that I had going on. Jerry Cutter and I had scheduled a meeting for the following week after the 4th and I always liked to prepare for those meetings in advance.

So as I'm talking to people, I was taking mental notes that I would need to jot down in my ledger. Stewart Sexton and Jerry Bobo from Nordisk were flying in later that month for a site visit at our Kentucky warehouse and I needed to make notes for that meeting, which I was also doing that night.

There was a problem with a Paxton Lumber shipment and a missing container which I hadn't tracked down yet. This wasn't unusual, but it was always a pain in the ass when it happened and usually it was just because someone made a mistake on a Bill of Lading or someone on the dock in Miami miscounted our containers. It didn't make my job any easier either way Tom Roberts from Roberts & Sons Billiards needed his shipment and I had to make it happen.

We had entered a partnership with them to supply the wood for their custom pool tables and sticks a few months earlier and though it wasn't a voluminous order, I still wanted to maintain the relationship and keep us on good terms.

My Mom came into town for the party and just seeing her smiling and happy, eased my mind a little. She had always worked so hard for us as kids, and I never forgot about that. Seeing her smile and happy was a driving force behind much of what I did. As fireworks exploded overhead, I tried to shut my mind down for a moment.

"Damn. I need to invoice Nordisk for Trucks...

Chapter 9.   Bracing For Impact

February 27, 1991, changed my life forever.

I started having night terrors soon thereafter and would often awaken in a sweat, with my heart racing, sometimes screaming after imagining myself having shot an American Trooper or being impaled by an Iraqi solider in a bunker. Catherine would calm me down and assure me that it was okay. She had never been to combat, but she had to watch me fight a different kind of war at home in her house.

I was emotionally ravaged. I wasn't ashamed at the fact that I had gone to war and killed the enemy. That was my job, and it was what I was trained to do. What we weren't trained to do though was deal with the emotional toll of the military lifestyle and war itself.

If you're constantly in a heightened sense of awareness and morbidity; walking on the razor's edge, you're bound to come out of it with some cuts and wounds that simply won't heal. They say time heals all wounds, but that's not the case with undiagnosed Post Traumatic Stress Disorder. Soldiers simply learn to cope and get through it.

Remembering my grandmothers mantra: "Smile and wave" helped me a bit.

Being an officer, further complicates things for soldiers. But a *young* combat officer can face even more mental hurdles to try and get over.

That was the burden that I carried with me. I replayed some of my actions over and over. My youthful leadership of my soldiers could have been better. I was harsh and un-accepting of simple failures. I had zero tolerance for just about anything that wasn't ready to go down range.

Of course, all combat line officer and NCOs would agree that being that way is *the only way.*

"Don't make friends, when in charge take charge and bring them all home safe."

That was my mantra as a leader. The way I went about it wasn't always perfect, but it was always because I had my soldiers' best interest at heart. That's why I had such issue with my leadership and how they handled my situation, and it changed my life forever.

It had taken me nearly 8 months for the night terrors to subside. By mid-1993, I started to get over the constant sadness that dogged me throughout my daily existence. I had poured all my being into CBI and my schoolwork at the University of Louisville.

One day, Dr. Lyle Sussman asked the students to discuss a hard life experience in his Human Behaviors class. I didn't think much of it. I got in front of the class started to explain my war experience and then I broke down. The class clapped.

No one knew, but I was in a tunnel most of the time; fighting day-to-day to try and figure out how to feel better. The hyper-vigilance was bad for social interaction but great for building homes, businesses and getting A's in every MBA class at the University of Louisville.

But would it be good for being a parent?

That was the crux of my thoughts as I sat there with Catherine one day. The "Is it time" question was really a "Am I good enough" question. But even more so, it was, "Am I healed enough?"

The questions poured from my soul as we sat on a wooden bench, wondering if it was a good time to start a family.

"Can I keep it together"

"Will I ever?"

"Will you go through this with me?"

"Can we do this?"

"Are we strong enough?"

For all the confidence that I displayed in my business, I was afraid of being a father. I wanted to be one, but I didn't want to make any mistakes. I wanted to be what I hadn't seen from my own dad when I was growing up. I wanted to be perfect.

Catherine listened to me. Studied me.

"Who really knows Adam, but we will do this together."

She was right. No matter what we faced, we were going to go through it as a team.

Meanwhile, back in Honduras we continued to do our tap dance of growth amidst limited cash flow. But no one was worried because no one really knew about our cash flow problems.

Nordisk was still there and so as long as they were placing orders and filling containers, we knew that we could make the system work.

Jimmy, however was worried about other things.

"It's dangerous out here Boss."

"Jimmy, there's nothing to be worried about. We are doing right by the people. They love us. We love them. You shouldn't worry so much."

Jimmy had been talking about how dangerous Olancho was ever since we first started our operations. I respected him immensely and trusted him with my life, but he worried too much to me. Things always came together, but Jimmy always seemed to be waiting on the other shoe to drop.

"There's a lot of money floating around out here."

"That's the idea Jimmy. We're trying to make money and I want to remind you; you are part owner of the company."

Jimmy chuckled just a bit to let me know he relaxed some. But it was far from being over.

"I've been hearing some things. This guy, Correra. He's got it in for you. He hates Americans."

"Who?"

I hadn't heard that name before and I wasn't kind of surprised to hear that someone may have had it out for me.

"He runs COHDEFOR."

The Honduran Corporation for Forestry Development or *Corporación Hondureña de Desarrollo Forestal*. I had seen that name on every damn document I ever had to get for our shipments and those scumbags were front and center when it came to extorting money from us for documents.

But I didn't know Sandoval Correra.

Two weeks later, Jimmy's intuition appeared to be right. I was in Honduras on a quick trip and one day this caravan of government cars rode into our lumber yard. We had been given a commendation by the Vice President of Honduras and we had amicable relationships with the local mayors and such, but we hadn't hosted any dignitaries at our facilities thus far.

When the gravel cleared, a short, Honduran man with a thick mustache and glasses, stepped out of one of the cars. He didn't smile and I immediately didn't like him. He didn't seem like he had good intentions.

"Mr. Rousselle."

Dad stepped forward and introduced himself.

I watched, quickly understanding his reasons. Dad figured if there was a problem, he needed to be the one to deal with it. The man with the mustache sized him up.

"You must be Joe."

He turned to me.

"And you must be Adam."

Dad and I shared a look.

"I am Sandoval Correra. Director General of COHDEFOR which is the Honduran Corporation for Forestry Development. It is a pleasure to meet you both."

"Likewise." I had spent enough years in the military to recognize a rat when I saw him, and this guy was a rat if I had ever seen one.

"How can we help you?"

Dad was determined to try and keep me out of this fray as much as possible.

"I just came to see your operation. You have been exporting quite a bit of Mahogany from our country. It's my job to make sure that you're following… the rules."

"We do everything by the books, and we have all of our documentation."

Dad didn't even try and schmooze this guy. I got the sense he didn't care for him either.

"You should know that."

I couldn't help myself. This guys and his cronies were taking our money and then he had the audacity to drive on to our lumber yard and act like he owned the whole damn place.

He smiled at me. But it wasn't friendly.

"I do."

Correra scanned the lumber yard.

"Is there something we can help you with?"

Dad had grown weary of this guy.

"Not at the moment. But I'll be back."

He climbed back into his car with his men and they left.

Dad and I watched Correra leave, knowing that this wouldn't be the last that we saw of him. It was August 2, 1994.

I wasn't sure of Correra's intentions, but I soon found out that Jimmy's sources might have been on to something. Correra oversaw all of the forests in the country. If it fell in the jungle, he heard it. If it fell at the hands of a foreign company, he hated it.

According to Jimmy, Correra had made it his personal mission to shut down a Mexican wood company the year before we got started in Honduras. This wasn't because he had some sort of noble cause to protect the environment either. It all boiled down to money. Correra tried to extort millions of dollars from that company and eventually they were forced to stop doing business in Honduras. Correra's victory was short lived however, as the Mexican Company sued the Honduran government and won! $11.6 million.

Correra's plan backfired and Honduras ultimately had to pay for over-zealous pursuits.

He had to repair his reputation. This guy was going to be trouble.

I gathered up all our documentation and information on IRC 936 in anticipation that something was going to happen with this guy.

Things at the company didn't slow, but instead were steadily picking up. Japan was becoming one of our regular customers and I had to work extra hard to keep up with them. Technology wise they were years ahead of us and were already using Lotus 1-2-3 version 5 and we weren't. To top it off, we were having issues with our Quick Books and had some items mis-entered which caused more issues as we tried to develop better Honduran cash flow expectations and budgetary information to determine how much debt the Rousselle's had in the business.

One thing that kept bugging me though was the overhead costs of our business with Nordisk.

We had to lower those costs to maximize our profits and part of that problem was having a better inventory of what was on hand. That way we could be more specific in our lumber needs in the jungle.

So I went to the International Hardwood Show to spark interest in our quilted Mahogany and Lignum.

I loved those shows. People loved veterans and gravitated to me. Our name had grown exponentially in just a short period of time, and I did my best to make sure we capitalized on our success.

I was energetic, charismatic, and always smiling when I went to those shows. People loved me. It seemed like everyone was saying "yes" to CBI.

The machine was literally humming. Our mills were going full throttle every day and night. There were a couple of hiccups with some shipments into Miami, but that wasn't anything new. We had dealt with that before.

On September 1st we received a letter from Sandoval Correra and COHDEFOR: "You must cease operations immediately for illegally cutting lumber in Honduras," it read.

Chapter 10. Frogs In Boiling Water

"This fucking mutherfucker cocksucker!" Dad's fax read.

I exploded by the time I actually read the letter from Correra. Dad had called and told me what was going on. This was total bullshit and we all knew it. WE had every right to be there, and we had followed all of the rules; to the hilt. I never once took a chance on anything. If Dad thought it was no big deal to be off by a couple of board feet on the lumber in the containers, I jumped on his ass big time about it. I could've been called a lot of things but first and foremost, I maintained CBI's integrity and followed all of the rules.

But Correra didn't give a shit. He already knew what my accounting looked like. He was trying to fuck with us. No one in Honduras cared for his ass and I'm not even sure why he was still in his same capacity after the Mexican company lawsuit, but he was there, and he was determined to get revenge on somebody.

Honduras was like that. "Come if you'd like, leave if you can;" the words on the sign leading into Olancho, wasn't about the people trapping you. It was about the laws. People made up their own laws and then enforced them at will. If someone wanted to accuse me of robbing a bank, all they had to do was tell the authorities that I did it. The cops would arrest me and take me to jail. No questions, lawyers, lie detector tests.; none of that. My ass would be guilty until I paid someone off to let me out and then it would go away. If they ever felt like arresting me again for the same bogus charges they would. They called it a "Notice To Appear."

I called it bullshit.

So Correra had trumped up some shit about us not being authorized to conduct business and we had to shut down. There was nothing we could do except wait to go to court, which was going to take two days. In the meantime, I'm still working to keep the business afloat. No one knew what was going on and I figured they didn't need to, because there might not have been rules in Honduras, but there were rules in the United States, and IRC 936 protected us.

I was right.

Two days later we went to court and the judge informed Correra that he in fact "does not have the authority or jurisdiction to shut us down."

He was furious, but we didn't care. I knew that we enjoyed the safety of a U.S. backed initiative in a foreign country. We were like the "Teflon Dons" of Honduras, except unlike John Gotti we weren't doing anything illegal. Everything with CBI was all by the books and on the up and up. We really had nothing to fear.

As we exited the courthouse, Luis's eyes squinted menacingly at Correra and his cronies. I had seen that look before. It was the same look he had given the men who had stolen he truck and brought it onto our yard that day. Dad and Jimmy knew that look as well.

Dad pulled Luis aside and whispered something to him that I could barely hear. "It's okay. We will handle it."

He patted Luis on the shoulders to relax him a bit, but Luis wasn't ready to relax.

Luis was a good man. A good family man. He loved his wife and children dearly and working for Gringo Joe, had afforded him the opportunity to better his family's life in ways that he could've never imagined. We paid him and it gave him the chance to send his kids to a good school; not some place in the middle of the jungle with dirt floors and raggedy or worse, no books. This same thing was true for so many of the people we hired to work for us. We were their ticket to a better life. But they did their part too.

They were honest and hard-working people. All they wanted was to know that their children and families would be in a better place in the future than they themselves might have been born into.

Correra and his antics threatened this for Luis and the rest of our workers. This wasn't something to be taken lightly. Correra didn't give a damn about them though because he was blinded by his hatred of Americans and his need to prove his worth.

Correra didn't know it or maybe he did, but he was treading in some very dangerous waters.

"I don't like that guy."

Luis glared at Correra again before we all jumped in the car and Dad popped open a bottle of Tequila to celebrate. CBI had just won our first court battle.

CBI didn't skip a beat. We picked right back up where we left off. It seemed like the flood gates had opened for our business. We began shipping to a Pakistani company late that summer, in addition to our already bustling Southeastern Asia clients.

The whole time Stewart Sexton kept asking me about our financials at CBI. I opened our books to him, because we needed their business. It was like he was trying to keep track of everything that we were doing at times, but I thought nothing of it. We had just shipped 17 containers for Nordisk and even though they hadn't paid us, I knew that they would.

"You oughta consider moving your shipping operations over to Maersk."

Stewart called me one day to offer his suggestion.

"For what. Seaboard has been good for us."

They had been for the most part. Sure, there were some occasional delays, but nothing unusual.

"CBI is growing and there's no limit. Seaboard can't keep up with that kind of business. They're cheaper and more reliable."

I respected Stewart's business acumen. He was an undisputed leader in the industry and our customer. I thought it was admirable that he wanted to help us save money,

"We need to drop our overhead."

Hernan Lleva, our CFO considered the question I had just asked him about Maersk. Hernan was a nice guy; native Honduran. He had come recommended to us from Judy Salazar at the Banco Atlantida and Dad and I both thought it would be a good idea to hire a respected local Honduran to manage our Finances. He drove this brand-new Mercedes Benz which in Honduras was a big deal. The workers would marvel at that car when he pulled up.

Hernan seemed to get along with everyone. Except Jimmy. Jimmy said he was a "snake" and refused to even drink coffee in the same room with him. We chalked this up to some more of Jimmy's island "Voodoo" shit and Hernan had shown himself to be trustworthy and reliable.

He seemed to waffle on the notion of using Maersk though, so I didn't press the issue. But he did have something else on his mind.

"Correra wants money."

"Fuck Correra!"

I wanted nothing to do with that guy. Ever.

"You don't understand Adam. He is a very powerful man. A very connected man. He can make things bad for you. For all of us."

"We've already won."

I refused to believe that crook could do anything to us.

"We won round 1, but Correra will win the war."

Hernan was stern-faced and direct. I dreaded asking the next question, but I knew I had too.

"How much?"

"He wants fifty grand."

"No way. I'd rather close this place down than to let that son-of-a-bitch get a piece of our money."

"A month."

"Are you kidding me. We have cash flow problems all the time and we're selling lumber out the wazoo. 50 grand will sink us."

Hernan opened some ledgers and pointed to some numbers.

"We've done well. You and Joe…"

"…My Dad and I have busted our ass for this company. For all these people. We aren't making nearly what we should."

"All I'm saying is it would be worth it, for us to pay this guy to keep him on our side. That's nothing compared to what it may cost us in the future."

I couldn't believe that I was actually entertaining paying off Correra. But I wasn't ready to make that decision.

"I'll think about it."

A few days later, Stewart Sexton called me to say that he no longer wanted any of our 2 Common Mahogany. I was floored.

"We don't need it right now. Just hang on to it."

THE MAHOGANY MAFIA

"Stewart that's a third of our inventory."

I could hear him breathing on the other end of the phone.

"Is it pricing?"

Dad and I had decided a few weeks earlier to increase our prices to Nordisk. It went from $1790 to $1840 per thousand board feet for the high-quality lumber and from $1450 to $1490 for the lower quality. Canahuati and Caoba De Honduras wanted it all for $1180.

Stewart hadn't bristled at this, but now he was effectively shutting down a major portion of our business. We couldn't afford to only do business with Canahuati at his prices and he had made it clear that he couldn't go any higher.

I had no choice but to bite the bullet and keep it.

We were screwed. We had people to pay and expectations to meet.

Stewart's brother, John Sexton worked for Hickory Chair. They were major purchasers of the 2 Common. The 2 Common was not the best lumber. It had these marks and dents in it, so there were only a few things that it could be used for. It couldn't be made into table tops, but you could make more legs; chair legs for example.

Hickory Chair would not buy high quality lumber. Not to be confused with usefulness. But now Stewart had told me that Hickory Chair wanted better lumber. Why would they need a clean and clear piece of board when all they're going to do is cut it into a thousand pieces? They don't want the 2 Common.

They backed up all my lumber which meant that my inventory went up. I couldn't keep it on my yard just sitting there. That lumber was literally money to CBI.

I did what I had to do.

I shipped it to the United States and sold it myself.

A Honduran company called Victoria Reproductions contacted me and asked about buying lumber. I couldn't figure out why they would want to do that. We exported lumber and they were furniture manufacturers. And to top it off they wanted it at the low local price! This didn't make sense. There were a lot of happening quickly that didn't seem to make sense, but I knew that we would get through it.

I got all the 2 Common Mahogany coming out of the jungle now. And I had to sell it myself at my prices. This meant that I didn't have the ability to deal with Michael Canahuati. We had shifted to using Maersk as Stewart had suggested and we had invoices that weren't being satisfied quickly enough. I had asked them to hold several shipments until we received the payments. Nordisk was one of those unpaid invoices and I kept having to bug Stewart to get the payment. They always came though, but it was just another layer that I needed to take care of.

We were in a cash flow panic.

Canahuati was in a panic of his own.

He invited me down to his place in San Pedro Sula and I obliged.

"Adam!"

"Hey Michael."

"It's Mike. We've been doing business for far too long for you to still be calling me Michael."

He was always a friendly guy, and I enjoyed our conversations and meetings. I got the sense that this one might be a little tense, but it wasn't.

Canahuati took me to his favorite Italian place, which was this, open air eatery just off the water. The food was absolutely delicious, and we drank wine and ate without discussing business for a while. It was still early, so he drove me to his furniture plant, and I was impressed.

He had built some operation, albeit from short-changing me on lumber, but that was my problem not this.

"Look at all of this. My family has been in this business for a long time."

"You've done well."

"Yes. We have."

He paused for a moment as he searched for his next words.

"Most of my family and the people that I know, do not trust American Gringos."

He sipped from the glass he was still clutching with his whiskey from the restaurant.

"But I have always been different than my friends and family."

He paused again, as if making sure I clearly understood what he was saying to me.

"I cannot let this business go under. I am asking that you continue to allow us to participate in my native country's industry."

"Of course."

I didn't hesitate. Canahuati seemed a bit surprised that I answered so quickly. But it was true. I was never there to try and get over on anyone.

Canahuati couldn't stop talking on the ride back to my hotel. We laughed and drank wine and whiskey until late in the night. It felt good to be away and relax for a moment.

If I knew what lie ahead, I may have never taken that visit.

Chapter 11. Gold Shotguns, And A Proposal

Dad had a nervous look on his face and I wasn't exactly sure why. Minutes before I had just told him about a strange phone call received from American Mining Corporation. They asked me if Dad was still alive!

"They want me dead."

He looked out of the window in the office as if to make sure no one was watching or listening to him. Luis was just outside with John on the sawmill and Jimmy was making his usual rounds. Everyone had something to do. We were always busy at his time.

"What do you mean? What's all this about?"

Dad leaned into me. He intentionally tried to wipe the nervousness from his expression and smiled.

"Belfate Mining Corporation."

He grinned and sat back. Satisfied that he had given me all of the information that I needed to know.

I knew all about Belfate Mining Corporation.

Hell Dad had talked about it nearly every day for most of my adult life up until that point.

Before I joined the Army and we were living in Florida, Dad had bought me a coin shop. In his mind it was going to be a lesson about business and "the world," in his words. I had zero interest in learning about "the world of coins," but I rolled with it. It was another attempt in Dad's long list of efforts to try and make up for the lost time he had missed in my life.

The shop wasn't fancy; in fact, it was tiny, but we were coin dealers, nonetheless, specializing in buying and trading gold and silver. Dad had immersed himself in learning about gold and one day this old man came waddling in.

He was loud and ornery from the start, reminding me of Al Pacino's character in "Scent of a Woman." His booming voice and commanding presence demanded attention. He started asking me all kinds of questions, each time raising his voice just below full-blown yelling level, ensuring I could hear him and understand that he knew what he was talking about. His questions were sharp and probing, revealing his intense curiosity and deep knowledge. Dad, ever the connector, quickly engaged him, and the two began to chat back and forth. That's what my Dad did—he connected with people quickly, effortlessly drawing them into conversation with his warmth and genuine interest.

"I know where the largest gold ore deposit is in in Central America," he shouted.

Was this guy deaf?

That's all I could think about as he continued. I could tell though that Dad was intrigued. He wasn't afraid to dive for Blackbeard's Treasure Chest, finding Ponce de Leon's Fountain of Youth, or go excavating for gold ore in Central America. It was just a part of his DNA.

"Where's it located?"

The Old Man looked at Dad as if he had fallen out of a tree, grunted, and left.

Dad and I looked at each other and shrugged.

"Old kook," Dad muttered.

That old kook showed up again the next day but still didn't reveal his secret. Then he came back every day for two weeks until finally, he was ready to reveal his secret.

"Honduras."

Dad's eyes widened like saucers. He had already been taking trips down there and he loved the country.

It turned out that the old man used to be a Senior Geologist for the U.S. Geological Survey as a surveyor of different foreign nations' assets. He discovered this gold ore deposit during one of his assignments. Dad was sold.

"I'll tell you what. Why don't we each buy our own plane ticket and if this is real, then I will pay for everything."

This appealed to the Old Man because apparently, no one had been listening when he had been trying to talk about this Gold Ore deposit in the past.

The two sealed the deal over a couple of nights of late-night Bourbons and good food.

They arrived in Honduras and the Old Man led Dad out to a deserted part of the country. Nothing was there except for this massive rock formation. He points in the distance and says "That's where it is." The two of them spent the next two days digging. It was hard work, but Gringo Joe was not going to be denied. Finally on that second day, they discovered a rock.

"It's right there."

The Old Man pointed to the rock Dad had just unearthed and sure enough they had found gold!

Gringo Joe had just discovered the largest gold ore deposit ever found in Central America. There was a huge news story done on him and his findings. Within months he formed Balfate Mining Corporation and investors flocked to be a part of the company. The Honduran Government granted him concessions. It was his with one very notable caveat.

"Under Honduran Law, that claim cannot be passed along to anyone," Dad explained.

"When I die it will become available for purchase to the first bidder. That could be you... or a powerful enterprise like the American Mining Corporation, who has enough money to buy anything they want."

That realization stung

Neither one of us said another word about it. The reality was that American Mining Corporation needed to keep tabs on Dad. His death was going to be their gain, and this had to be unsettling, even for someone like him.

It was for me.

Especially in a place like Honduras where money could buy you anything you want; including someone's life.

Business continued to roll, but Nordisk was becoming more and more inconsistent with their payments. I started working with Maersk's U.S. shipping office in Cincinnati. It seemed like they would be a great fit for CBI and Stewart Sexton had been right. We were a little over a year into our business and we were only $119,905 in debt! That was it. Still, cash flow was tight, and inventory was growing at an aggressive rate, like a virus, beautiful and ominous at the same time. I was doing my best to keep selling the 2 Common on my own, but I felt like a hamster running on a hamster wheel. The faster I ran, the further away the end seemed to be.

Though we had transitioned over to using Maersk instead of Seaboard we had another shipment held up in Miami. We couldn't figure out what was the issue this time. The containers had been packed perfectly and our Bills of Lading were all correct.

Dad got a call one day from a gentleman named Michael McKee from Commercial Affairs at the U.S. Embassy in Honduras. It was the weirdest thing. We hadn't spoken to him before, as far as we knew, so the call was strange and out of place. He inquired about how business was going and if we had any problems. Dad assured him all was well. He didn't bother to mention the $50K that Correra was extorting from us.

I would have told him.

I mentioned the held-up containers to Stewart Sexton one day during a phone conversation about our profit margins. He kept asking me about how much money we were making and when I told him our current debt, he was impressed.

I mentioned to him though that the changes in his ordering patterns were causing a strain on the company. He listened and assured me that we would figure it all out. He had another idea though.

"You should consider shipping your lumber via break-bulk."

This was a method where you simply loaded the wood directly into the hold of the ship, rather than put the wood into containers and then on the ship. In theory, it allowed you to ship more lumber and thus lower your inventory quicker, which would mean that CBI could get paid faster as well if Nordisk adhered to our agreement.

Stewart noted that if we were shipping on the boat instead of shipping in containers it would save a lot of money.

"It would be easy; you just load all of the wood onto the ship."

We spoke about determining the amount of lumber that would fit on the ship.

"Map your lumber yard's inventory and use that as a guide," he suggested.

When we hung up, I weighed Stewart's suggestion. It all made sense. The only problem was if I did that, I would move all our lumber out of the U.S. Free Trade Zone and into the Honduran economy where the U.S. laws didn't apply.

I reasoned that wasn't really a big deal because the lumber would only be there for the time it took for the ship to be loaded and set off.

I calculated a very small risk but figured who would want the lumber anyway.

This all weighed on my mind as I traveled back to Kentucky. Dad had insisted on going to Florida and we were going to meet back in Honduras at the airport in a couple of days. He said he needed to go and see his American doctor and Catherine and I were planning a vacation to Paris. It would be our first real vacation that didn't evolve around work meetings and wood conferences. I was excited.

Dad and I had planned on spending three days in the States. Right before we were scheduled to leave, I got a call from Hernan Lleva.

"Our containers in San Pedro Sula have been impounded."

"For what?"

"I don't know. Seaboard is just not a good company?"

What?

We had been with Seaboard for months and now suddenly Lleva tells me "They aren't a good company." Per Stewart's suggestion, I had started using Maersk, but we hadn't switched over completely.

I couldn't help but wonder why Lleva hadn't mentioned this before. It was bad enough that the containers had already sat there for two weeks but now they were being impounded? I was baffled. Dad nor I had any good answers.

I arrived back in Honduras before Dad. I grabbed a car and parked it near the front of the airport and walked back in to meet him at Customs. When he rounded the bend, he was pulling a golf bag with stuffed animals nagging out of the top of it.

"Adam!"

He was jovial and happy, and I figured he had a good visit aback in Florida; probably visiting one of his old girlfriends and friends. He hadn't brought that golf bag with him though, but I figured he was probably bringing a set of clubs back to Jimmy. Dad and I would do things like that for everyone.

He used to bring stuffed animals, perfumes, and games for Luis's family all the time when he traveled back to the States. Most of the stuff he'd give away, and the rest he'd sell. He didn't have to do it. I think Dad just enjoyed the idea of it all. He was kind of like some sort of Marco Polo, traveling to the Far East or in this case, Florida and bringing back exotic gifts, like... golf clubs and teddy bears.

Dad stood in line, and I waited at the Customs counter for him. He finally got to the front, still joking with passengers, and laughing. The Customs Officer took his passport and looked him over. He had seen Dad before.

"Gringo Joe."

Dad smiled. The Man didn't immediately smile back. Instead, he looked directly at Dad's golf bag.

"What's in there?"

"Clubs. Stuffed animals for my friend's daughter. She's turning 8."

The Officer looked closer.

"Empty it out."

Dad looked at me and I shrugged. He grinned sheepishly.

"Sure thing."

Dad emptied the bag and pulled out what must have been 10 pink elephants. The animals lay on the floor. The guy half-heartedly looked at the gifts, seemingly disappointed. He tapped the side of the bag and felt the clubs.

"You can go."

I helped Dad load up the stuffed animals and we left the airport.

When we went to Honduras, we would often rent out a suite that could accommodate the two of us and Jimmy if he wanted. It allowed us to relax a little in the city while also being able to conduct business. We often kept our cash in those rooms and it's a wonder no one ever tried to come and rob us. But then again they knew the consequences.

When we got back to the hotel room, Dad poured himself a drink and gulped it down. Then poured another. He turned to me, with a huge shit-eating grin.

"Get those god damned stuffed animals out of my bag."

I thought nothing of it and began to toss the animals out. He jumped up to help me and when I had finished, he threw the bag on the floor and started pulling out shotguns he had wrapped in tape and taped to the inside of the bag!

He had a damn arsenal!

There were six shotguns total in there. I had a fit.

"You could've gotten arrested!. I'm a respected U.S. Army Veteran. Do you know what would've happened if you had gotten caught?"

I was beside myself. Dad had just jeopardized everything that we had worked so hard to build.

Dad looked at me and poured himself two more drinks.

"Nothing."

He drank his third drink.

"What are you talking about!"

I was still pissed.

"Do you think I was about to pay those customs crooks $500 to turn the other way?"

I was confused.

"That's all it would've taken. $500 dollars. Those assholes would've pretended like they hadn't seen anything."

Dad sipped his drink and then looked at me. There was silence.

And then we both burst into laughter.

Gringo Joe had struck again. The shotguns he explained were for his protection and then he planned on making a "couple of bucks off the others."

What could I say?

When I got back to the office, an entire sales team from Maersk called me.

"Seaboard is ineffective. Everyone knows this."

Everyone except for me.

I listened to their sales pitch. I was frustrated and drained over the whole ordeal. In the end, I chose to use Maersk as our sole shipping partner. Stewart called me soon after that phone call.

THE MAHOGANY MAFIA   89

He had another idea for CBI that was much bigger than anything I could've ever imagined...

Chapter 12. Every Decision Has A Price

"You know what Adam? I need a vacation. Why don't I come down to Honduras in a couple of weeks and you can show me around? I've been wanting to visit Honduras for a while now?"

"Sounds good."

"And maybe you can show me your business operations down there. So I can get a good feel for how you do things."

Stewart Sexton *already* had an idea of how we did things. That was part of the reason he had proposed that CBI should function as just a sawmill so that we profited only from cutting the lumber and not from actually harvesting it. I considered the idea briefly and made a note of my own. Doing this would essentially eliminate a portion of our business. That didn't make sense.

I decided that I would counter Stewart's proposal with an idea of my own, to establish a fixed rate with Nordisk for 3 years, guaranteeing that we would continue to do business with a required minimum of over a million lumber feet.

Stewart arrived in Honduras a few days later. I picked him up at the airport and we had dinner and avoided business talk. It was great conversation, mostly about the cultural nuances of Honduras and its people. It was a good night.

I picked him up at 7:30 the next morning for breakfast and then we headed to our facility in La Ceiba. Stewart was immediately impressed, just as he had been months earlier when he had seen our inventory in Kentucky.

"How did you find your local employees? How much do you pay them? Have you had any problems with theft?" What are your profit margins?"

The questions were endless and I gladly answered them for him.

I introduced him to every aspect of CBI. Our employees explained how we harvest trees, why the employees are important and our unique relationship to our local People.

Stewart then introduced Nordisk to our leadership team, and we all had a discussion of the CBI business plan. Stewart and I delved deeper into cash flows and the net present value of CBI. He was truly impressed about our low debt ratio.

"You have done well here Adam."

I knew he was right. We had done well. And to think this all spawned from a challenge from one of my M.B.A. classes at the University of Louisville!

When we were done, Stewart offered to make a $425,000.00 investment into the operations of CBI Lumber.

I was confused. A few days earlier, Stewart had talked about CBI working solely as a sawmill and now he wanted to invest in our company. I asked Dad his thoughts and he couldn't quite figure it out either. But Stewart wasn't done.

The next day Stewart asked to buy half of CBI Lumber for $850,000.00 paid out over 3 years that Nets $540,000. He proposed that I could sell 5% of my stock for $75,000, issue 50% new stock, sell Nordisk a total of 55% and they would get 5% vote after 3 years on the deal.

My head was spinning. I hadn't gotten this far in my thinking yet. I had no idea that they wanted to *buy* any part of the company, nor was I prepared to sell it. Stewart sensed my hesitation.

"There is another option as well."

The second option was for me to sell Nordisk preferred stock for $350,000 prior to close. CBI would then lock in the gross profit at 18.5% with a preferred stock option convertible to common. I would retain the vote of 50% for the first three years and $350,000 debt-free. There would be 6 members on the Board of Directors; 4 of them mine. They would have no salary for me, just a cut of the profits.

"How does that sound?"

"*How does that sound?*"

I didn't know how the that sounded. This was my first company. I had no real answer.

Stewart boarded his flight and left, and I still had not made a decision. The problem for me in all of this is that I didn't understand the offer, and why he made it and I had no one around me who did.

I explained all of this to Hernan Lleva, my Dad and Jimmy and no one had any insight. Lleva instead mentioned something about those assholes at

CODEFOR, which only pissed me off as I thought about the $50K we had to pay those crooks to let us operate. I hadn't bothered to mention that to Stewart Sexton. I figured that as a bigger corporation, he would be able to circumvent Correra and his crew.

Our meeting got cut short because Michael Canahuati started blowing up the office telephone. Just like that. Out of the blue. I was surprised that Stewart hadn't mentioned him or even invited him to our meeting. Canahuati had already told me that they sort of knew each other. But I also figured that Stewart wouldn't want Canahuati to know about his proposal to me.

Canahuati asked if we could cut the wood in different dimensions than the usual 8/4. What the hell! Why would he want to do that? He was a furniture guy. I pushed back and he said he needed to have the wood at the other sizes for a big client. This was going to slow down our operation.

It was weird. Stewart Sexton wanted to buy CBI and Canahuati was trying his best to shorten our profits. In the end he kept coming with these bizarre demands about different species of wood that he wanted, and that with his business as I understood it, he really had no business asking for them. I needed to get back to the States and see Catherine, so I eventually relented. What else was I going to do?

I loved coming home to Kentucky. Though I couldn't sit for long because of my hyper-vigilance and busy work schedule, there was a certain tranquility in Elizabethtown that was refreshing and rejuvenating. This intended to last me for a couple of days and then I'd dive back into the rat race again. As a young guy, I was doing older man work, learning on the fly, and "smiling and waving" at everything that came my way.

Catherine and I talked about Stewart's proposal and ultimately, we decided that we weren't ready to sell CBI yet. We could see how valuable it would become in the future and Stewart's proposal wasn't the best fit for now.

The timber industry didn't come with medals or commendations, but its price was just as steep. I had learned in both love and war that loyalty wasn't just about standing firm in the easy moments—it was about sitting through the worst of times together. Sacrifices made for those who trust you are the currency of leadership, and every choice demanded a payment

"No problem Adam. The offer will stand."

His "good 'ol boy" accent always made you feel like he was the sincerest person you could ever know. I didn't think he would be upset, but I was still happy that he took it so well.

"I know this is bad timing, but we have a problem with our shipment in Manning, South Carolina."

Stewart still sounded friendly and upbeat.

"What's going on?"

"We have bugs in the wood."

Damn that wasn't good. Every so often we would have shipments that had these bug infestations that had to be exterminated before the wood could be off loaded. It wasn't frequent and Stewart assured me that it should be handled in a couple of days. In the meantime, though it would delay our payment.

If he had paid us at the time of shipping, the lumber would not have sat around and none of this would have happened!

Stewart assured me this had nothing to do with our decision to not sell a portion of CBI, and I believed him. Why wouldn't I? That lumber had been sent to Manning weeks ago. It was just a coincidence and no need to worry. He promised to call in a couple of days, which he did and we received our payment.

I needed to make a quick trip to Germany to see my old friend Peter Weiss, from Theodore Nagle. I figured I would squeeze it in at the end of the month, come back to Kentucky for a week, and then Catherine and I would fly to Paris for our vacation. I stayed in the office late one night working through the details when I received a call from my dad.

"I need a favor."

"Okay. Sure. But I'm not smuggling any shotguns into Honduras."

We both chuckled.

I listened to his request., and then told him, "I'll do it."

"Are you crazy?"

Catherine thought the whole thing was loony from the start.

"We're always having cash flow issues."

"I know. But Dad has worked hard for CBI and he doesn't ask for much. Ever. I want to do this for him. I *have to* do it for him."

I looked at her and she realized that I was serious. I had to do this for my Dad. He wasn't perfect and he screwed up a lot of things in my life, but as an adult, he was there for me every step of the way since I left the Army.

"I'm going with you."

Dad wanted a boat.

In fact, he had already found one. I'm not sure how and he didn't reveal to me exactly how he had found it, but it was a 44-foot Marine Trader located in Pickwick Dam, Tennessee. It was a 4 ½ hour drive from Elizabethtown. He found this guy who had a boat that he was selling and without ever seeing it or investigating it, Dad had decided he was going to buy it for $50,000.00.

"I want to retire and live on the Tennessee River on that boat."

That's what he told me on the phone. I felt like he deserved it and though I had no clue who this guy was or if there even was a boat, I was going to do my part to make this a reality.

I called up the guy and we agreed to meet a gas station in Pickwick Village. I withdrew cash from the bank and Catherine, and I set out to go and put a down payment of $5,000.00 to buy Dad's boat.

The guy was shocked to see me when I arrived. I introduced myself to him and shook his hand. I asked him if he had the boat and he said yes.

"Well it belongs to Joe Rousselle now. Thank you so much."

I proudly handed him an envelope with the cash in it, signed the option agreement to buy it and he couldn't believe it. He told us the boat would be there when Joe was ready for it. Catherine and I grabbed a quick bite to eat and headed home into the late October evening.

"Do you think we'll ever see that boat or that guy again?"

"I hope so."

I really didn't know.

I was beginning to feel like every time, Stewart Sexton called, I would enter into some sort of bizarre world. And I was right.

"Adam, we'd like to buy some Two Common."

"But I thought you told me you didn't want any more of it?"

"I know, but we've had some of our customers ask for it. Do you have any of your inventory left?"

"Sure."

I got the feeling that Stewart was less concerned about buying the Two Common and really trying to figure out who I might have sold it to.

"I didn't sell anything to any of your customers."

I wanted to clear the air and make sure there was no misunderstanding.

"I wouldn't do that."

"I didn't think you would. We just need to get the Two Common."

I assured him I would get the wood for him, but it still left a bad taste in my mouth. I had scrambled to find buyers for that lumber because our biggest customer didn't want it. Now he wanted to buy it again. When would we get paid? What issue would be next? I was pissed off and upset. Stewart was affecting our business. Correra and his guys were robbing us. The community leaders. The activists. They were all draining us, and Nordisk wasn't helping. This shit had to stop.

I picked up the phone and called Hernan Lleva.

"Screw Correra. Don't give him another penny."

"That's not a good idea Adam."

"Screw him. He's hurting our company."

"We're fine Adam."

"No we're not. He's a crook. I don't care how much money we make, we're not paying him anymore."

Hernan went silent. I could hear the reluctance in his breaths. But I was right. He didn't understand how I detested being taken advantage of. It was one thing to pay "toll fees" on mountain roads, or even "taxes" for passing through a town. It was robbery to pay a government agency that much money, and I had made up my mind.

Whatever Correra wanted to do, I would be ready.

Chapter 13. Reflections In Paris

I couldn't get out of the door fast enough. Catherine and I were all set to leave for Paris, and I had calls coming in from everywhere. It was organized chaos—the best kind of chaos, filled with excitement and anticipation, and it was the best moment of my life.

Catherine waited patiently until I finally finished answering questions and jotting down notes. Then the phone rang again.

"You might as well answer it."

I grabbed one final call as the cab waited for us and it was George Tate from Home Depot. Home Depot wanted to start acquiring garden fencing with all our lumber scraps. George framed it as, "We want to help ensure that CBI is reusing all of its lumber and being environmentally friendly," since we had so much Mahogany scraps and leavings that normally would be thrown away. Home Depot wanted to turn those into picket fencing for gardens with little staples and pieces of plastic behind them to bind them.

I hadn't thought much about reusing the lumber. In my naïve thinking, I thought that there was an endless supply of lumber and never considered finding a use for scraps. I had falsely taken nature for granted.

I thought it was a great idea that people would be so thoughtful about saving the environment with little pieces of unusable wood that we had. I did find it odd though that in their quest to be "environmentally friendly," they were using plastic to bind the pieces together. I didn't have time to debate it though. That wasn't my battle to fight.

Paris was amazing as we thought it would be. We didn't spend much time sightseeing, but being away was exactly what I needed.

Even though I couldn't stop thinking about work.

Back in the States, I desperately needed to do some financial reconciliation. We had outstanding orders from Nordisk that needed to be paid immediately. Being away for a few days had allowed me to consider our relationship with Nordisk and Stewart Sexton. I really couldn't understand them. The whole bit with the Two Common had put us in a pinch and I needed to let him know that. Not to mention that he wanted us to change our role in the relationship.

I decided that my frustrations needed to be put into writing.

"Stewart, we started this relationship to create value. Now you're claiming that CBI could be vertically integrated. In your fax you mentioned trust. I make projections and spend money based on your purchase orders then you say you're buying less. It's hard for us to have trust when you make these kinds of moves. You mentioned that there was a problem with the quality of the wood we shipped to you. How could this be possible. You have two of your inspectors at my mill, who okay the grade of wood that we ship to you. I need to have a warm fuzzy about this relationship again. I don't know when and if I will get paid. I need a measure of good faith. How do I know you will honor this new agreement you're asking for a tall order cut to a certain size packed a certain way shipped at a certain time in a certain order to a certain place. Do you understand what I must do and what we have done to produce these special orders? This is not Burger King. I brought you to Honduras, opened my books. told you I would not pursue your customers and have not. You ate at my dining room table. Indeed we need to address current claims of poor quality but this issue must be addressed according to normal industry standards and not determined from standard operations Where do you think a 29 year old disabled veteran gets the cash to do business of this magnitude from a bank? No. We don't. How do you expect me to explain to my investors why I am negotiating to reduce a current purchase order of 46 containers valued at 736 thousand dollars to 22 containers valued at $350,000 A net LOSS OF sales of $380,000. I want to know what you're going to do to get this relationship back on track. I could make a case to reduce the current P.O. to a lesser amount if I could be convinced that over time the reduction is beneficial. I need some measure of your good faith one all claims you have now. I need you to prepay the next 2 containers and give me a purchase order for March and April."

I didn't know how Stewart would take the letter, but I felt like it had to be written. He called me a few days later to let me know he received it and he would make sure that we received all of our necessary payments and he sincerely apologized for any "misunderstanding" on their ordering.

I was relieved the letter had gone over so well. But Stewart wasn't finished.

"Things change quickly," he reminded me.

"You know Adam, we actually need more Two Common for a new customer in the Philippines. And we'll come in at the higher rate you discussed."

"How much do you need?"

"They want 30,000 board feet."

Damn!

In December of 1994, business was booming for CBI. The prospects of selling 30,000 board feet to Nordisk for their customer was going to give us a strong start to 1995.

"We can do that."

Of course, Stewart already knew that we could do that. That's why he brought it up. It was an olive branch of sorts for CBI and Nordisk.

"Good. Have you had a chance to do anymore research on break bulk shipping? It's just so much cheaper."

I had.

Stewart had mentioned shipping without containers several times in the past few weeks and I had tried my best to block it out of my mind. I wasn't sure why; maybe just because it was something different and anytime you change things up you never really feel comfortable.

"I think we can do it."

I gave him my answer. It was time to shit or get off the pot.

"Great. I knew you would come around."

Our conversation once again shifted to questions about our cash flow and profits. Stewart was always seemed amazed by the sheer volume of lumber that we shipped, and he always kept saying "You gotta fucking be kidding me" in that thick, Southern twang that he and his brother had. For a New Yorker they were the epitome of "good 'ol boys" with those accents and John's "aw shucks" demeanor.

When I hung up with Stewart, Maersk called to see how things had been going. The timing was perfect. I had more questions about break bulk shipping, and they were eager to explain the process to me and offer packing suggestions. This really seemed like it was going to work out well for us.

News traveled fast in Honduras and Judy Salazar from Banco Atlantida called us about increasing our line of credit. She had heard that we had struck a big deal with Nordisk and imagined we would need more cash to help out.

This was music to my ears. They could see that CBI was destined for several lucrative business opportunities and wanted a part of it. Life was good.

And Catherine was pregnant!

As I drove form the office, to Walmart, I visualized what the process would be: lumber from the jungle to the warehouse, packed onto trucks and then... "We needed a flatbed." I made a note to call my Dad and Jimmy when I got back. I had to finish my Walmart run.

Luis had just had a brand new baby. He was ecstatic and now that Catherine and I knew we were going to have a child, I felt a strong urge to buy something for the newest addition I picked out some clothes and toys for him and grabbed a few bottles of Aqua Velva for Luis. It wasn't expensive, but they didn't have anything like that in Honduras and Luis loved it. Luis was such a good guy, I loved doing things for him and his family.

Dad and Jimmy let me know we needed more than a flatbed and I started doing the math to figure out how we were going to shuffle around money to buy the supplies we needed. We had deals happening, but still cash flow was an issue. That was just the nature of the business for us; and it was only intensified because we were still in relative infancy as a company.

Southern Edging, the company that was working with Home Depot on the picket fences, was already in production and demanding more scrap pieces. It wasn't a ton of money, but we liked their business. Theodore Nagle, Yao Leun, The Koetters; everyone was actively buying from us. We just needed cash.

Stewart Sexton sent a fax to my Dad asking for dimensional wood. We typically did not do this. He wanted 3" x 3" and 4" x 4" square pieces of lumber and they wanted the square pieces of lumber to put on a lathe and make wooden legs for chairs. They wanted several containers, and I told Dad to do it.

Michael Canahuati called to place a big order soon thereafter. He wanted: two containers of One Common, five containers of Two Common 8 foot only, five containers of One Common 5/4 and four containers of 6/4 and three containers of 10/4 for a total of 19 containers! Luckily, we had received a payment from Nordisk and our cash flow issues were okay , *that day*.

I began to get anxious because I knew that we were about to be in a real cash crunch. A few more orders of this size and we could once again be in scramble mode.

And then this happened…

Stewart Sexton faxed back and said he now wanted the lumber we were selling to him to be kiln dried!

Kiln dried? Was he serious?

I figured this had to be an error because we didn't even own a Kiln!

"Stewart, I think there's an error on one of your orders. We don't own a kiln."

CBI did not dry lumber. The closest Kiln was at Caoba de Honduras but that was three hours away. And I wasn't sure that I wanted to send my lumber to him and pay for that.

"I know."

You know?

I was dumbfounded.

"Even if we did, since that process takes 45 days, that would kill the cash flows we have worked hard to establish."

"Nordisk will write a letter to the bank as a good faith declaration, that you can use to get an increased line of credit."

With an increased line of credit, I could probably look at building my own Kiln on my yard. I couldn't say no to that.

In the meantime, I would use Canahuati.

Stewart sent over the letter verifying that we had a business arrangement, but he didn't mention Caoba de Honduras. He said that CBI would kiln dry the wood, but we didn't have a kiln. He knew this. The bank asked me what to do and we had to get Stewart to rewrite the letter for us to get the increase.

A week before Christmas, Stewart asked us to ship 25 containers of Selecting Better Mahogany to New Orleans. That pushed us over the top. I called the bank to get some help with cash flow. Our orders were getting bigger and bigger. This was the price of a booming business in the lumber industry. I talked to Judy about this, but she said we needed to have the letter from Nordisk.

I sent Stewart a note: *"The problem with the letter of credit is unresolved. We are not in the business of kiln drying lumber. You need to fix the letter of credit or we can't ship you the lumber because you know it's not dry."*

Christmas was unlike any that Catherine and I had experienced before. We were going to be parents and we were able to host our family and friends for the holidays. We had traveled the world in 1994 and we were excited about what the future held for us. Catherine declared that we would have a boy and before I could say anything, she said it, "Adam."

Two days later, Nordisk canceled the letter of credit and agreed to wire $200,000 by the end of February.

Chapter 14. Treachery

I didn't know why Nordisk chose to cancel the letter of credit. I tried calling Stewart to follow up with him and got no answer. I tried calling Michael Canahuati as well and couldn't get him. These guys were like me; we didn't take days off, so I wasn't sure what was going on.

Finally, Canahuati called a couple of days after Christmas.

"Adam, my friend. I'd like to order three shipments of door-jam-sized wood."

It was odd, but I had become accustomed to Canahuati and his requests as of late. I agreed to do the shipment and didn't think too much of it. I wanted to make another trip to Honduras before the end of the year but had decided I would wait.

As New Year arrived in Kentucky, I sat down to write down my goal for the upcoming year. Ever since my days in the military, I kept track of everything that happened to me each day. Every meeting, phone call, order, potential customer; everything. But now instead of my trusted green notebook Sgt. Sparks had given me, I had my Franklin Planner.

"I want to grow a business from all of the lumber scraps and support of Home Depot by maximizing the use of all of the bits of wood that we would never ship for lumber."

Simple enough I thought.

January started with a bang. Maersk was holding several of our containers in Port Everglades, Florida for some reason and I couldn't find out why.

But it was worse. I got a call from the U.S. Department of Labor stating that the Social Security number of one of the Americans we were paying wasn't working and I needed to verify the number. I had no idea what that meant.

I checked with our HR person and the number came back to be for Alex.

Alex was a great guy and he and I got along really well; probably because we were the two youngest people on staff at CBI. We would spend hours at this wonderful little thatched roof, ex-pat bar in La Ceiba shooting the shit while eating fish, and this macaroni salad that reminded me of the good times at home when I was a kid. That salad was incredible. No matter what, I always made it a point to go there when I came to Honduras and it was all because of Alex.

Alex was my friend and this business about his Social Security number didn't quite add up. On my last visit to Honduras, Alex and I had walked into a thatched hut in the wilderness on our way to one of the places where we would buy some lumber. It was on a dirt road, and I had a terrible, terrible, headache so bad that my left eye was closing.

Alex had suggested I stop in the hut and tell the lady about my headache. He had heard of her and thought she could help. Without hesitation, she walked outside of her hut, went over to a bush, and started massaging the tree.

Alex nodded reassuringly at me because I had this "What is she doing" look on my face. She came back in, and she sat near the mud stove that seemed to dominate the room. That stove emanated comfortable heat and kept the whole hut warm.

She opened her hands and laid these green balls, which I assumed she had gathered from outside, on a pan and started to mash them with a wooden mallet. They sat there on that red hot mud stove until they started to smoke.

She then swept them off with her hand, shook them inside of her two closed hands, and cast them back on the mud stove like a set of dice. All I could think was *Is this some voodoo shit I'm witnessing?"*

Alex smiled and nodded, which I believed to mean that he had somehow heard my thoughts and was confirming my suspicions. Those balls stayed on the stove for what seemed like hours. This wasn't helping my headache.

She then swept them into a stone bowl and mashed them some more. Then opened the tall pot on the stove and poured all the now-dark mashed green balls into the water and it boiled. She finally turned back around and looked at me for the first time since she had walked outside to that bush.

She flashed a warm, three-tooth smile and said "Café!"

"Gracias."

My Spanish was never particularly good, but I could communicate enough to let people know my thoughts.

She had made me coffee for my headache. We were at a high altitude and added to that some dehydration; that was my problem. I hadn't even thought about it. It probably had something to do with Alex and me visiting the bar the two nights before this trip.

She made me the simplest remedy for my headache; passed down through generations like some gift from heaven. She seemed to pour her soul and her family's love into the coffee that she prepared for me. But she wasn't done.

She began to talk to me about life, joy, happiness and kindness through generosity and selflessness.

"Remember, you do not know everything in this world. Continue to marvel at all that you see and hear."

She poured me a cup of coffee, in a white ceramic cup, taken from a high beam in the hut, where it had sat upside down ornamentally for years. She had deemed me worthy of it and smiled with pride of someone sharing their most precious possession.

My headache went away, my heart soared, and my mind opened. In that moment she gave me strength for that day. Alex was happy that I had met her.

"She has a gift."

I could only nod as we left, and then as I sat there reflecting on what I had just heard about Alex from the Department of Labor, I was afraid he was a phony.

I hoped that I was wrong, so I called Dad to find out how we could've gotten Alex's Social Security number.

"Damned if I know."

Dad didn't seem too concerned with Alex's situation. Bigger things were going on.

"A couple of our drivers got arrested."

"For what?"

"Because we're rich."

Dad's sarcasm held boundless truth. Being arrested in Honduras was a common place thing. Over the year we had several workers "arrested" for supposedly committing nonexistent crimes. All it took was for someone jealous or upset to file a complaint against you and "BAM." The cops would arrest you, extort some cash from you, and more than likely the judge would throw the case out. It was a hassle more than anything.

We always paid for our workers to be freed. That was another one of those costs of doing business, but it seemed that this was starting to cost more and more.

"I think we're being watched." I could tell Dad was smoking a cigarette as he spoke to me. I imagined he probably had a glass of scotch nearby.

"By who?"

"I don't know, but this guy keeps coming by the warehouse and saying that we owe him money."

"Anybody know him?"

"Not really, but I think he is planning something."

Dad was right. Something was being planned.

A few days later five more drivers got arrested and their trucks were impounded. We had to pay $20,000 per man to get them freed! I was pissed. We were bleeding money that we didn't have. Nordisk's wire hadn't come in yet and Canahuati was always slow on his payments. We had to make some changes quickly.

"We got shot at. They put two bullet holes in the side of the truck."

Dad didn't sound frightened, but he sounded alarmed enough for me to know he wasn't bullshitting.

"I'm coming down."

It took me a few days to get there, but when I arrived in Honduras at the Hotel Paris in La Ceiba, Dad and Jimmy were talking a mile a minute from the moment I got to the hotel. We went up to our suite.

"Boom. Boom." I heard it and luckily, I didn't let go of the wheel."

Dad was standing up and reenacting how he and Jimmy both had to duck down to keep from being hit by an assassin's bullets.

"This is no game Adam."

Jimmy had that serious look on his face. I had heard this before.

"So who was it?"

Jimmy and Dad shared a look.

"We obtained a warrant for those responsible. Hernan Lleva, me and Jimmy testified,. They're in jail. All of them. Mutherfuckers."

This *was* serious.

Obtaining a warrant against someone in Honduras meant that they would have to go to jail. These were these rotten open-air prisons, with no real sanitation, except for one toilet in the middle of the cell. The food was horrible and the conditions were deplorable, to say the least. Though you were "in jail" you could sometimes leave if you knew the right person or paid off the right people. These guys weren't rich, so they weren't going to pay someone off, but they certainly knew people.

By obtaining this warrant, we had thrown ourselves into the local culture in a way that might come back to haunt us.

"There's something else, I have to tell you."

Dad stepped aside. Jimmy rolled up his shirt sleeve and looked me directly in the eyes.

"His name is not Alex. He has been lying to us all along.."

Jimmy had snuck into "Alex's" apartment while he was gone and found his passport. "Shit."

I didn't have a whole bunch of time because I had promised Catherine, I would be back in time for us to go to the University of Kentucky basketball game at Rupp Arena with Michael Ream and his wife. They had invited us as their guests and we had never been to a game before. Going into Rupp was a Kentuckian rite of passage. It was like going to the Super Bowl every time Kentucky played.

I hopped on the flight and the whole time, I couldn't stop thinking about Alex, or who I thought was Alex.

I tried to call Maersk again about our containers that were held up in Port Everglades because they had been there for a long time. I finally got a hold of someone and found out that the containers were being held up but it had nothing to do with Phytosanitary.

This was the environmental inspection to make sure there was nothing in the containers that would harm the environment. If this wasn't it, then what the hell was the problem?

I called the F.B.I about Alex. I didn't know what the hell he was mixed up in or what he was doing. I spoke to a local agent who gave me the rundown.

"Yeah, we know about him. That's why we're inspecting your containers in Miami."

Holy Shit!

The F.B.I. wanted to see if we were involved in a drug ring along with Alex. I couldn't get off the phone fast enough.

"He's wanted for drugs or drug related charges by the F.B.I. They've been crawling over our containers for a long time and they thought we might have been shipping drugs."

"What the hell!"

I could've said a lot of things about my Dad, but he did not indulge, support, or transport drugs in any way. He did not support that shit and was violently against those who did.

I called the F.B.I. guy one more time.

"What can I do to help you arrest him?

"Nah. We don't care about him. He is small time. We're not going after him. He's a two-bit guy in over his head and screwed up and got caught."

I was relieved to hear that and even happier to hear that our containers were going to be released. As much as I liked Alex, I knew that it was over. I was saddened by this, but I got on the next flight to Honduras.

Dad, Jimmy, and I confronted him together. As soon as he saw us, he knew what was up.

"Thank you."

There wasn't a whole lot that he wanted to say, and we understood. Alex had been a hard worker. He was reliable and respectful and always showed up on time and did what he was supposed to do. We were going to miss him.

"Here."

I handed him an envelope full of cash.

"Good Luck to you."

Dad hugged him first, which spoke volumes for how much he liked the guy. Jimmy and I were next. We shook hands and then left.

I thought about going down to the old bar and grabbing some mac salad for old time's sake, but there was just too much work to do at the moment.

Stewart Sexton and Nordisk wanted shorter pieces of wood and Yao Leun was ordering more and more Guayacan Sanctum to be shipped to Hong Kong. I had trips lined up all over the world, Catherine was pregnant and back in Louisville, the city had asked us to expand our operations there.

As I climbed back into Dad's minivan, I couldn't help but notice the two bullet holes in the driver's door. Dad had been lucky. The warrant had stopped the extortion attempts and arrests for a few days, but it was all about to start again soon, and this time someone from CBI's executive team was going to jail.

Chapter 15. Turning Point

"Do one thing and only one thing. When you do a second thing people won't trust you even if you can do both. It doesn't matter what you think, it only matters what they think, and be careful, when two people say you're drunk, lie down."

Jeff Bracker from the University of Louisville told me this when I went to tell him about what was going on with CBI. Everyone had all these ideas about what CBI should do; how we could expand our business. Someone even asked us to make charcoal out of the old pieces of wood. Hell, we were already doing fencing with Home Depot. I wanted to grow, but I also wanted to be careful in our direction. It was exciting and exhausting.

I took Jeff's words to heart. But there was one area we did need to get involved in: kiln drying.

Nordisk had already mysteriously asked us to Kiln dry the wood they wanted even though they knew that we did not have the equipment to do so. I got to thinking and John Salazar and I came up with a plan. We decided we were going to buy the equipment and have it at our sawmill.

This would keep us from having to transport it to Canahuati in San Pedro Sula, and save on our costs.

I made it clear that if we were going to do this, I was only going to buy the equipment from my old friends Tom and Jerry Koetter, to be fair to them. John began talking with Jerry Renneker who worked at Koetter and also did some selling for us. There was a problem though.

Our cash flows were low because of the change in the letter of credit from Nordisk and the requests for all the different sizes and shapes of wood with Nordisk and of course our payments from Canahuati, who had just ordered 15 containers of all kinds of shit.

It was great to get all these orders, but when they all came at once and everyone had special requests, it crippled us in a way. We had to use all our cash to keep the business going and thus buying that sort of equipment wasn't feasible.

So on Catherine's birthday, we went to visit the Small Business Administration to see about taking out a small doc loan. We knew we could pay it back as we always did all our sort of "in-between loans" since the business was growing.

Dad had called and said he needed more supplies, particularly guns. This wasn't unusual, since he always needed guns, but he wanted 10 and I figured he was still uneasy about his minivan being shot at.

"Still trying to meet you down in Honduras Adam."

Stewart had been calling me daily to see when I might go down to Honduras again. He kept saying it was important that we meet there. I was irritated with Stewart but tried to remain civil and professional. He had put us in a bind again and to top it off we had 11 containers of his wood en-route to the United States as we spoke.

I didn't know when the hell we would get paid for that either.

I ran through my calendar. Decided that I would go down there on the 25th of January.

"Perfect. How's the shipment from San Pedro Sula."

"Good."

I had agreed with Stewart to ship this order of 11 containers form Puerto Cortes instead of La Ceiba as a "dry run" for our decision to use "break bulk" shipping for Nordisk's orders moving forward. The truth was it made sense to not use containers if moisture was not an issue for the wood, which it wasn't. The containers were no longer technically in the U.S. Free Trade Zone, but I knew it didn't matter. We were a protected American company.

The day I was about to leave for Honduras, I got a call from David Warford a lumber broker and Reggie Vachon from Jay Gibson McElvain a lumber company and a buyer from Gibco Holdings. They wanted to issue us a letter of credit each month for 400,000 board feet of lumber now with 11,000 board feet in a container. That was basically our facilities' entire production at that time! I delayed my trip for a day to try and figure out those details and got a call from Dad.

"They're saying some shit is going down with us."

"Who is they? I haven't heard anything, and I'm supposed to meet Stewart in Honduras tomorrow."

"Some of our workers have been grumbling about it. Said that they're trying to screw us over."

"Who?"

"Correra."

"Screw Correra. He's a snake. We have done everything we are supposed to."

"I know. I'm just telling you what I heard. We'll talk about it tomorrow. When I get there."

"Did you ship the guns?"

"Yes. I shipped them."

Dad and I hung up.

That guys' name never went away. I knew that he had been pissed about CBI refusing to bow down to his requests for money, but legally he had no recourse. I checked my faxes and notes just to be sure, and there was nothing.

Rumors were not uncommon in La Ceiba or Olancho; especially when it came to the prospects of money being lost by our workers. I had heard so much different shit that I had learned pretty quickly how to discern truth from paranoia. But this didn't sit well. For Dad to call me about this news, meant that there could be some truth to it.

I called Hernan Lleva, who always had a pulse on Correra's inner workings and got nothing. By the time I hung up, I had nearly forgotten about the proposal from earlier.

When I arrived at Customs in Honduras, Stewart and another gentleman, whom I hadn't met before were waiting for me. Stewart smiled big when he saw me and seemed to be proud to introduce me to the guy, whose name was Tom Rashford. We shook hands and began small talk as we approached the Customs Agent. Stewart and Tom passed through with no problem, but as I handed over my passport, the Agent stopped and motioned to another guard nearby. I could see Stewart quizzically watching, trying to determine what was going on.

"Everything good Adam?"

"Sure thing. Everything's fine. You go ahead and I'll meet you at the hotel in a little while."

"You sure?"

"Positive."

Stewart and Tom left and I waited for the guard to finish inspecting my passport.

"Come with me please Mr. Rousselle."

"What the hell is going on," I thought.

I hadn't done anything wrong, and I had been in and out of Honduras at least 100 times in the past year. I wasn't worried, but I just couldn't understand what the holdup was.

They led me to a room and searched my bags and inspected my passport again.

"Sorry about that."

And that was it. They let me go. I never did figure out what the whole holdup was about, but I didn't have time to ask. I needed to catch up with Dad and Jimmy in our suite.

"They don't just stop guys like you at the airport. Trouble is brewing Adam."

Jimmy looked me squarely in the eyes.

"You need to get out of here."

"I'm not going anywhere Jimmy. They let me go. I'm an American citizen and an Army Veteran. I'm not afraid of shit."

Dad joined in.

"No matter what. Don't you give up what you have worked so hard to build."

I studied his face in between plumes of smoke from his nearly finished cigarette. He was already reaching for another one.

"Look guys nothing's going to happen. Relax."

Dad nodded to Jimmy.

When we arrived for dinner and drinks with Stewart, he seemed shocked to see us.

"Adam. I see everything worked out. What happened back there"?

"Nothing. Just a little mix up at customs. It's Honduras. Shit happens all of the time."

Stewart nodded slowly.

"Yeah shit does happen all of the time here."

Several of the locals kept coming up to Dad to talk to him and soon we were all laughing and having drinks. Through the haze of drinks and the horns of the live band playing that began to fall on all of us, Stewart and Tom leaned into me at the table.

"What do you think your total inventory in Honduras is worth at this moment/?"

I knew exactly what it was worth because I always made it a point to keep accurate details of our inventory and cash flows.

"$10 million. With more coming in daily."

Stewart and Tom looked at each other and then at me.

"That's fantastic!"

I took a sip of my drink and smiled back. Yes, it was fantastic.

The next day, I took Stewart and Tom back up to the mill. When we arrived, John was on the phone with the Koetters discussing the Kiln drying equipment.

Business seemed to plug along as usual. Stewart took a moment to show Tom some of our inventory. I had planned on meeting with Hernan Leva to discuss some of our financial issues, but he wasn't at work.

"Where's Hernan?"

John shrugged as he talked on the phone. No one else seemed to know either.

It was January 27, 1995,. From where I stood things seemed normal. Trucks were rolling in and out of the yard and the sawmill was buzzing. Jimmy needed to go back up to Olancho to check on things and Dad was busy overseeing some of our workers loading a container.

I had to go to Japan in two days because there were two companies there who wanted to buy some of our lumber, and Dad, Jimmy and I were going to ride up to the ranch in Olancho together and come back that night.

"We have to head to Olancho later. Do you want to come?"

Stewart had not been in the jungle yet and since we weren't going all the way into the trees, I figured this would be a good time to show him what we had there.

"No. We're going to be getting back to our hotel. We have to leave soon." Stewart and Tom left just as Hernan pulled up.

He got out of his brand-new sports car that he had just bought two months earlier, smiling as usual.

"I had to see Judy Salazar at Banco Atlantida."

"What did she say?"

"She said that they would be willing to loan us additional money for the purchase of the equipment."

"Good."

I didn't bother to bring up my concerns with the Nordisk shipments and cash flow with Hernan. Dad and Jimmy were waiting and I needed to go.

I always loved driving through Olancho. Just seeing the people and the joy that they had with the simplicity in their lives. They weren't bogged down with mortgages and car payments or even credit for that matter. All that they wanted was to see their children get educated and be able to make a better life for themselves.

Since finding out that Catherine was pregnant, I found myself often wondering what our baby would be like and what he or she would think of their dad one day. I had seen my own father evolve into a person that I wasn't sure existed. I had come to appreciate his mannerisms and respect his business sense and decision-making. I wondered as we drove through the winding roads deeper into the mountains, would my daughter or son one day find me as equally complicated and redemptive.

Things were humming along at the Ranch as usual. The trucks were loaded to cart wood to the sawmill.

"I told you there's nothing going on."

Dad and Jimmy had spent the drive up to Olancho trading stories about their experiences in Honduras and reminding me that we should be sure to keep our eyes and ears open for any sort of foul play. I laughed at the stores and halfway listened about Correra. I couldn't stand that guy. He represented all the parts of this beautiful country that I wished weren't there.

By the time Jimmy finished in Olancho it was dark. We considered spending the night at the Ranch, but that meant we would've had to get up before dawn for me to get back and get to the airport to go to Japan.

No one, including me wanted to do that, so we decided to make the drive back.

"I know a shortcut."

Dad always knew shortcuts. He was the king of shortcuts through small towns and villages in the Honduran jungle. I laughed to myself as I imagined him in Pathfinder School. Driving through the jungle was one thing. Hiking through the woods with only a compass was something entirely different.

As we drove along the road we arrived at an armed checkpoint. This wasn't unusual because they were scattered across various roads. Some were "legitimately' operated by the Honduran government. Others were set up by local villagers who would run fences across the road so that they could stop trucks to rob them or demand fees for passage.

Dad pulled up slowly to the gate and the guard came out of his office which was a small building, big enough to maybe house 10 people. He was armed and didn't seem too happy we were there.

"Where you going?"

"Just driving."

Dad could be a smart ass when he wanted to.

The guard shined his light in the car at me and Jimmy. Looked at us suspiciously.

"What's your name?"

"Joe Rousselle."

The guard looked squarely at Dad. He went to his shack and came back a moment later with his weapon drawn.

"Get out the car!"

Dad put his hands up and got out and the guard ordered me and Jimmy to get out as well. He led us into this enclosed room that only had one door that was semi blocked by his desk, which he moved to let us walk by. He ordered us to sit down in a chair and picked up his phone to make a phone call.

"I have a man named Joe Rousselle here with two others."

We could hear him talking. Jimmy kept translating for me.

The guard hadn't bothered to ask me my name.

He hung up the phone and came back and sat down in front of us and drank from his coffee mug. All of a sudden, Dad began laughing loudly. It startled me and Jimmy as much as the guard.

"You're a stupid mutherfucker you know. Do you realize how much fucking shit you are about to get into?"

The guard looked at Dad strangely. As if he didn't understand him or believe that he was actually talking to him. He was armed and we weren't. Well Jimmy was, but the guard didn't know that, and it was late at night on a dirt road in Honduras.

"I'm talking to you mutherfucker. Don't just sit there like you're fucking stupid. You dumb ass!"

Dad continued berating this guy, and all I could think was "What the fuck are you doing?"

But he wouldn't stop laughing and talking shit to the guy.

"You have no idea who you are fucking with. I will fucking kill your stupid ass right fucking now. I don't give a shit about you."

Dad couldn't stop.

Finally Jimmy stood up. He had heard enough.

"You need to let us go right fucking now or in a little while some American guys are going to show up and they are going to slit your fucking throat."

The guy looked at me and then at Dad. Jimmy had gotten his attention.

Jimmy had that Caribbean English accent that made him sound like British Royalty to most Hondurans. Though they generally dismissed Blacks there, those that spoke the "Kings' English" were often granted immunity and given special considerations. Jimmy and the guy looked at each other. Then Jimmy withdrew his weapon and held it in his hand. He didn't point it at the guard, but he let him know he had it.

THE MAHOGANY MAFIA

"In ten seconds we are going to fucking leave. You do not want to piss these people off."

Jimmy tucked his pistol back where it was, in his waistband on his back.

I was dumbfounded. My mouth must've hit the floor.

We walked toward the guard until we were just inches away from him. He looked around and then moved so that we could pass.

We walked out of the office without looking back once and climbed into Dad's car. The guard walked outside and slowly opened the gate. Jimmy nodded to him, and he nodded back.

"Works every time."

Dad and Jimmy laughed heartedly despite our circumstances. It was the second time I had been detained in the past two days in Honduras.

The next morning as I made my way to my gate at the airport, I had this strange feeling that someone was going to come up to me and stop me at any moment. I had never felt that way before in Honduras. I had always felt safe; diplomatically protected. But that day I felt different.

When I boarded. I smiled at the flight attendants as I usually did on these trips. I took my seat and opened the shades to look out at La Ceiba. I had come to love the city and it held a dear place in my heart. I met so many wonderful and kind people there, whom I genuinely cared for.

As the plane taxied down the runway, I began to jot down notes in my notebook. I thought about the surprised look on Stewart Sexton's face when I showed up for dinner. I wondered why he was so concerned with coming down to Honduras. Then my mind quickly turned to Nordisk and their recent requests. I began scribbling a letter that I was going to fax to them when I arrived in Japan.

Trust, I had learned, was the glue that held any operation together, whether in a combat zone or a conference room. Respect was earned not by titles, but by showing up when it counted. In this jungle war, as in every battle I'd fought, resilience and a dependable team were the only way to survive a turning point. Betrayals would come, but so would victories

As the plane finally lifted into the air and banked left, I turned to look out of the window at the sunrise over the mountains. I had no idea that I would never see Honduras again.

Chapter 16. Honduras Is Burning

It was January 30, 1995. I had been in Japan for roughly a day and half and all my meetings had gone extremely well. I was excited about the prospects.

The phone in my hotel room buzzed with a sense of urgency that is unmistakable the moment you hear it.

"The mutherfuckers confiscated our containers in San Pedro Sula."

Dad's voice sounded distressed and angry at the same time.

"For what?"

"Not sure. The letter doesn't say. Just that they are being inspected."

"Fax me a copy."

Dad sent the letter over to me and sure enough, it didn't say why the shipments were being held.

My guess was because it was such a large lumber shipment and we hadn't been shipping from San Pedro Sula before, so they needed to make sure everything was in order.

We had all our inventory and Bills of Lading, so I didn't bother to notify Nordisk at the time. I figured this wasn't a big deal, but I did call our offices in Honduras, to see if anyone had heard anything.

Nothing.

Dad had asked me to wire $32,000 to him in order to cover payroll. Banco Atlantida had put a hold on all our payroll checks which meant that some of our administrators didn't get paid. This had to be resolved immediately with Banco Atlantida, but I wired Dad the money in the meantime.

The next day when I arrived back in Kentucky, I called Judy Salazar to get this all corrected. We negotiated terms for our loans, even though nothing was overdue and ultimately decided that all loans would be due in 90 days, which I didn't foresee as a problem. By putting a hold on our checks, I felt that Judy had affected our reputation with our workers. Everyone knew that we always paid them on time. I had to drive this point home to her.

"Do not ever do that again please. Our workers are our greatest asset."

Judy agreed and made mention of some sort of oversight. Still, the whole thing left me a little leery.

I contacted PNC Bank in Kentucky and arranged for CBI to get a "bridge loan" for $45,000 to be paid in 60 days. PNC also offered to do a line of credit with us. I then used that loan to wire money to Judy Salazar to have for Hernan Lleva on behalf of CBI.

I was so busy trying to make our financials make sense that I couldn't even give much thought to the fact that Sandoval Correra had publicly accused Dad and I of shipping illegal lumber in Honduras.

This was such bullshit and just another of Correra's ploys to get money from us. Dad, Jimmy, and I got on the phone to discuss what our next move should be.

"This is such bullshit. They need to release our containers."

"He wants money."

Jimmy was angry.

"We're not giving him anymore."

"What do you want to do?"

Dad asked the question, because he was willing to do whatever, we needed.

I played with my thoughts in my own mind before I said anything. I was always so confident about our position in Honduras because I knew I had one move that could combat any of Correra's bullshit.

That move was to contact my Kentucky Senator and creator of the Caribbean Basin Recovery Act, Senator Mitch McConnell.

I knew that Senator McConnell would not take too kindly to hearing that an American company was being bullied by a Central American Country who had relished in the economic boost his Act provided. I always admired Senator McConnell's work and from every indication he was personable and open to constituents. I didn't need to tell Dad and Jimmy this yet though.

"Let me think about it."

Correra's claims had no real effect, except to attempt to undermine the integrity and reputation of CBI. It was ironic that Judy Salazar and him had both opted for the same tactic, though Judy's intent was never to harm CBI. It was simply to "protect our professional relationship." Correra's efforts once again did nothing to stop us.

In the meantime, I began crafting a letter to Senator McConnell explaining our plight in Honduras. I wanted him to somehow intervene so that we could finally put all this behind us.

But before I could really get into the letter, Catherine and I had a sonogram done of our new baby. I can't describe the feeling of knowing that there is someone whose entire existence is directly because of you. I could have stayed at that hospital all day looking at those images, but we couldn't. Kagiya Lumber in Japan wanted to purchase some domestic lumber, so I needed to get Jerry briefed on the details. We had samples to send out and I needed to get a hold of someone in Honduras who could tell me what was going on with our containers, because no one would.

I spent days chasing my tail on this with no results. I was frustrated because I wasn't there to deal with this in person, but it wasn't an option. Jimmy called me a few days later with news I had never expected.

"Murder? Of who?"

I could barely grasp what Jimmy had just told me. A rush of anger swept through my body.

"Joe's been accused of murder."

I couldn't believe what I had just heard from Jimmy.

"The environmentalist Jeannette Kawas Fernández."

"That's such bullshit!"

I was screaming at the top of my lungs and Catherine rushed into the room.

"What happened?"

I paced back and forth trying to make some sense of this. I knew this was another ploy to extort money from us, but this was bad.

"He said it to the newspaper."

Jimmy continued. His voice was strained, and I could tell he was pissed too. Jimmy wasn't one to mess with when he got mad.

"Who ?"

Jimmy paused for a moment.

"Correra."

I slammed my fist against the wall.

Jeannette Kawas was a popular activist throughout Honduras. She was beloved by the people and even though she fought for the protection of the forest, she had never said anything about CBI, nor accused us of any crimes.

She was the president of the Foundation For The Protection of Natural Resources of the regions of Lancetilla, Punta Sal and Texiguat (PROLANSATE). She rose to prominence by reporting cases of illegal logging, attempts by individuals and private entities who had tried to illegally seize the Punta Sal Peninsula, and cause damage to the National Park and other protected areas. Some of her enemies didn't like her because she opposed some economic development projects that negatively impacted the environment.

She had been murdered a few days earlier on February 6, 1995 at her home in a place called Tela, Honduras.

Jeannette Kawas was a good person.

Her murder would not go unavenged and who was an easier suspect than the "greedy" American who had made a "fortune" off of their lands. Correra's false accusation was a death sentence and I had no doubts that he knew that when he said it to the newspaper.

"Where is he?"

"I've got him somewhere. He's safe."

"Has anyone there mentioned it to you?"

"No. Everyone here knows it's Correra's bullshit games. They're pissed. Something is going to happen."

Jimmy was right. Something did happen.

I got word that Honduran Congresswoman Victoria Contreras had gotten involved in whatever was going on with our shipment in Puerto Cortes. She was known to work blatantly with Judge Rubeana Galeano to use the judicial process to eliminate political enemies and rivals by having them imprisoned, without release dates. She was bad news and apparently, she and her judge friend, had decided to focus their attention on CBI. The word was that

Contreras called for a special Congressional commission to investigate CBI's problems supposedly for the negative impact that CBI's closing would have on the workforce.

That sounded like it was beneficial to us, but it wasn't. Contreras could give a shit about us being shut down illegally, this was to see how she could benefit from us closing.

I had to scramble. The Honduran government was aiming to shut us down and with Correra on one side and Correra on the other side, the walls were closing in.

I contacted our friends at the Honduran President's office and didn't get any real information. The only thing that they told us was that Sandoval Correra did not have the authority to shut us down, but that didn't make me feel any better. I knew that they could possibly be in on the whole thing, and I didn't trust them anymore. My belief that we were safe was waning by the minute, but I knew that Mitch McConnell would be able to help us.

Dad and I spoke every day. He had come out of hiding because the press had disputed Correra's claims about him being the murderer and begun to bombard Correra himself with negative press. He was being plastered all over the media as an inept and irresponsible government official. I know this incensed him, but I was glad that Dad was okay.

"Do you remember what I told you?"

Dad asked me this question out of nowhere but I knew what he was talking about.

"I won't."

"You built his company honestly and with nothing but good intentions in mind for these people. Fuck them. Do not give in. No matter what."

"I won't."

"Promise me."

Dad and I had long since stopped making promises to each other. It had to be a direct result of my childhood when he would promise to come and see us, and never show up. I didn't hold that grudge against him, but I guess there was something that made sure I never put him in a position to make a promise to me, nor would I allow myself to make a promise to him. I would just do it.

But this was different.

THE MAHOGANY MAFIA

"Promise."

"Shit's going down tomorrow."

We hung up without me getting any clarification on what that shit was, but I knew it had to be something big. And it certainly was.

The next day, hundreds of CBI employees stormed the highway that linked La Ceiba to San Pedro Sula and the Puerto Cortes. They tossed mounds of old rubber tires in the middle of the freeway and set them ablaze, effectively shutting down all travel between the two cities.

They had had enough. Correra's tactics had worn on them, but more importantly he was fucking with their livelihood. They knew what his next step would be and that was unacceptable. If he had shown his face anywhere around them, he would have been a dead man.

Dad and Jimmy kept me abreast to every move of the people. Jimmy said the smoke was so thick that he couldn't see the airplanes taking off from the airport anymore. He was right.

They couldn't see them because they had stopped. CBI employees had created such a disturbance that it was unsafe for planes to take off and land at the La Ceiba airport.

I witnessed this with my own eyes. CNN ran a brief report about the fires in Honduras that stemmed from a "labor dispute." It was a short video piece, but we had made international news!

As I watched the thick plumes of black, smoke billowing into the air, I couldn't help but think of 4 years earlier to February 27, 1991 and my time in the Iraqi war. There was something about seeing that destruction and understanding the fear and angst that those people felt without knowing what the future might hold for them. This was life and death for them. Those old memories rattled in my mind as I watched.

The government was desperate and contacted us to see if we could intervene with our workers. I spoke to Victor Tiller in the President's office and he expressed what I deemed to be a sincere interest in fixing all of this and helping us come to a peaceful conclusion.

"Correra is a wild man. He has no rules," he advised.

I already knew this.

"We just want our containers back."

"I will work on getting your 15 containers back, if you will work on ending all of this. It doesn't look good for any of us."

"It was 11 containers."

Tiller seemed confused by this. He looked at me quizzically, but kept his thoughts to himself.

I agreed with him. The negative press wasn't going to be good for any of us. If CBI was going to somehow get through this, I knew some of our customers might be skittish going forward if they saw what was going on.

When we hung up, I realized for the first time that we needed a lawyer. I contacted the Kentucky Bar Association looking for referrals for someone who might be experiences in International Law. They promised to get back to me.

Dad and Jimmy managed to settle things with our workers. I had promised everyone that we would honor our agreements and pay them for that month, and I fully intended to keep that promise.

Two days later, Sandoval Correra demanded that CBI pay him $40 million for undervaluing our lumber shipments and illegally exporting lumber out of the country. He had employed a phalanx tactic against us. Corruption, murder, lying; you name it. His idea was to discredit us in any way possible and then hopefully something would stick.

Two days later he said "If Joe Rousselle would come down to San Pedro Sula he would drop all charges and give us back our containers.

"Bullshit."

He wanted us all to come down there so he could arrest us and put us in jail forever. He had no jurisdiction where Dad and Jimmy were in La Ceiba and he was helpless. We ignored the scumbag, but time was not on our side.

Dad was in need of oxygen and would have to get it soon.

On the final day of what had been a tumultuous month of February, I called my Mom to wish her Happy Birthday.

"How are you Adam?"

"I'm great Mom. How are you?"

"I'm happy. The flowers are beautiful."

THE MAHOGANY MAFIA 125

"I'm glad you like them."

"Adam, don't forget, smile and wave."

That night I attended another University of Kentucky basketball game. I did my best to hide the stress and emotions that I felt. I hadn't come this far to turn around and I wasn't going to.

On March 2, 1995, CBI was shut down permanently by Sandoval Correra.

Chapter 17. Surviving On Borrowed Time

"What's the plan?"

Dad, Jimmy, and I all had the same question.

My heart began racing as I thought of the trickle down effects of CBI being shut down: Catherine, our new baby, our house that we had just taken out a 2nd mortgage on to help cover business expenses, Dad, Jimmy, our staff. *How could I have let this happen to everyone?*

It wasn't my fault, but as a former Army officer and someone who had dedicated my life to try and take care of and protect others, I couldn't help but feel some sense of guilt at all of this. As all Officers know, you are responsible for all that happens and fails to happen.

But those feelings had to subside because we had to figure out what we were going to do.

On March 2nd, out containers that were being held in San Pedro Sula were inspected. Based on this inspection, which was utter bullshit, the Honduran government with Sandoval Correra and Victoria Contreras leading the way, seized all of CBI's operations. Contreras then filed a lawsuit against CBI for not being able to pay our employees! But worse, Correra filed a warrant for testimony against Dad, Jimmy, and me.

Sandoval Correra had stacked the deck and he was holding all of the Aces. The charges against us carried life sentences in one of Honduras's open-air prisons. I bristled at the thought of it.

Dad was arrested a few days later. He had been picked up outside of the La Quinta hotel where he was living.

Argentina de Batras was the first to call me. Dad knew that he would probably have trouble reaching me, so he called her and she called me.

She and Dad were still married, as far as I knew, but he had taken up residence at the hotel because her family was still not too sure about "Gringo Joe." The bullshit press and planted stories by Correra and his crew only added fuel to their suspicions. Being thousands of miles away, I felt helpless.

"They want $9,000 dollars and they will set him free."

THE MAHOGANY MAFIA   127

Hernan Lleva had spoken to someone who was connected to Correra and managed to get Dad's "bail" money reduced to $9,000. Luckily for Dad the newspapers had wreaked havoc on Correra's claims that he was involved in Kanawas's murder or he would've never gotten out of the place. In fact, it was discovered that apparently, two Honduran officials were implicated (though none were ever arrested): Colonel Tire Amia and Sgt. Parodol and a third man by the name of Mario Pineda.

Dad and I had met Pineda in a bar in La Ceiba one night. He kept asking us "What do you do?" no matter how many times we answered him. His name stuck with me, because there was something about his eyes that seemed empty and hollow to me. It was a look that I had seen in some of the eyes of Vietnam Veterans who struggled to maintain their sanity when I was in the Army.

It was the look of a solider who had killed someone.

I wired the money to Honduras and Dad was released from prison.

"These mutherfuckers are not going to stop."

Dad's voice fluctuated with each word. He was coughing heavily and wheezing when he spoke. I could hear Jimmy talking in the background, saying something about the workers and payroll.

Even though we were shut down, I had already determined that I was going to pay everyone at least through April. I was secretly hoping that this would all be resolved somehow by then and we could get back to business as usual. But in my heart, I knew this was impossible. We had reached the point of no return. In order to pay everyone, I had to ramp up our domestic business. Kagiya in Japan was actively moving towards purchasing Red Oak from us and I had tried to put Jerry Renneker in charge of the account, while I called up everyone else, I could think of. Jerry wasn't introducing himself as an employee of the company for whatever reason and I had to meet with him in order to get it all straightened out.

Eventually we worked through it and moved forward with the deals. Yao Leun had always been a loyal customer and I sent them a new pricing list of what we had at our Kentucky warehouse and listing for our American selections. I contacted QVC, Southern Edging, Lowe's, Home Depot, K-Mart, Walmart, Theodore Nagle in Germany and gave them all new pricing lists.

I even met with a Taiwanese company and a group of investors to potentially look at landing some sort of grant. I was desperate, but no one in CBI knew what I was going through.

"You have to leave Honduras."

I had already begun looking at getting Dad a place to stay in the states. Honduras was dangerous for him. I knew that they were going to come and arrest him again, whenever Correra got a whim up his ass to do so. But his health was declining too.

"I'm not going anywhere. I live here."

"Yeah, but we have to get you to the doctor. You need more oxygen right?"

He paused. This was true, as much as he hated to admit it. His trip back to the states had been interrupted by the fires and everything that was going on.

"Now is the best time to leave."

After whispering something to Jimmy that I couldn't quite catch, he agreed to come to the states.

Dad was in bad shape. He ended up being checked into a hospital in Florida, but at least he received good care. I couldn't even get down there to see him, because I was hopping flights from Kentucky to Atlanta, and everywhere in the East to find business. In between trips I was taking doctor visits with Catherine and seeing our son Adam, on sonogram. Things were happening fast.

I still hadn't updated Nordisk about the extent of what was going on and oddly enough Stewart Sexton hadn't been calling as much as he had prior to our containers being held up. I knew this was odd, but in a way, I felt some sort of relief that I didn't have to deal with his questions at the time.

"You have to protect your personal assets."

My attorney Jay Tanner stated directly as I sat across from him in his office in Louisville.

"You're getting behind in your payments. They've shut your business down. It's just a matter of time before you find yourself over your head in debt. And then what?"

"I cannot file bankruptcy."

I hated even uttering the word. Jay had just mentioned it to me moments before. I didn't even know what bankruptcy meant. All I knew was that for 7 long years, you can't get a loan, you can't buy a car. Can't buy a home. Can't do anything. It was The Scarlett Letter.

If I filed bankruptcy we would lose everything we owned, including the house that Catherine and I both loved so much. Plus, I needed a place for my son to come home to.

"Look I'm not telling you to file bankruptcy right now, but you need to seriously consider moving your assets and shutting down CBI completely."

That notion stung like hell.

As I drove away from his office, I kept replaying these scenarios in my mind of what bankruptcy would look like. I hated the thought of having to tell Catherine that our dreams had been stolen and there was nothing that we could do about it.

In the end I decided that we weren't going to file bankruptcy.

I sat down and began calling even more intensely than I had before. I worked the phone and fax machine like I had done a year and a half earlier when I was first getting started and didn't quite know what I was doing. Now though it was less about people taking chances on an unknown Army Vet, and all about the relationships I had built in the industry. I had a strong grasp of the power of networking and referrals, and I used it to my advantage.

Kagiya had sent specifications on flooring lumber that they wanted and because of our relationship with them, I was able to get meetings with Sado Sone with Nichinan, who was one of Kagiya's customer. This led to two other meetings with Ikegami and Nan-in.

By the time April rolled around, we had enough money to cover payroll as I had hoped. But there was more.

Dad had been discharged from the hospital and despite my please and disagreements, he refused to stay in the United States (as I knew he would).

"What did the doctor say at the hospital?"

"I have some problems breathing."

I already knew this.

"What else did he say?"

"Said I might be coming down with something.":

"Coming down with something?"

"it's really no big deal. No need to make a fuss about it."

"Are you sure?"

"Positive. Me, Jimmy and Luis are gonna go and check everything out when I get back."

I had no reply for this. We still had our staff on site in La Ceiba, but there was nothing we could do. They were essentially just sitting there. Waiting to get paid. I wondered how did the guys in the jungle react once they heard that we had been shut down.

No one except me grasped the gravity of our situation. All we had was our lumber on the yard in Kentucky. That was it. When it ran out, we were finished.

Dad went back to Honduras, but had a problem when he went to go back to the room.

"Hello Mr. Rousselle. We need to bring Mr. Rousselle's account current."

In all of the hectic and frenetic movements of my life, I had forgotten to pay Dad's La Quinta bill.

I quickly paid it and told Dad to be careful. But that didn't mean anything to him. And I knew it.

The next day he called to let me know that everyone was in still at the sawmill and were grateful for being paid.

I met with Jeff Bracker from the University of Louisville a few days after my conversation with my Dad and he made it abundantly clear that I needed to make a change.

"Is Honduran lumber the only kind of wood you can sell?"

"Of course not."

"Then that is your next business. You may not be a manufacturer, but you're damn sure a great salesman."

Jeff was right. The blueprint was in front of me. All I needed to do was run with it. Screw Correra. He couldn't stop us, even if he was holding our shipment hostage.

But first I needed to do a real personal financial reconciliation of my personal expenses. I didn't have much debt, but I did have creditors and investors who needed to be reimbursed. Not to mention there were orders that hadn't been filled for Honduran Mahogany. Some of those payments had been received; particularly Nordisk.

I needed to figure out how much overhead I needed to start a trading business. According to my calculations, I needed to build a good viable business with monthly sales of $108,000. Profits near term should be $45,000 to $50,000 a month. But I had to ask, if we reorganize how long to make profit is this the correct method of thought? I thought about creating an entirely new corporation, but protecting my family was number one and I wasn't sure this was the best route.

I had $92,000 in cash. I had $260,000 in debt and I had a $170,000 house, $23,000 in a lot in Kentucky and $50,000 personal equity; equaling $240,000 in assets. That meant I had negative $20,000 in equity

This was going to make it nearly impossible for me to receive any sort of loan from a traditional bank.

"Can creditors take our assets?"

"Yes."

Jay Tanner's reply was quick. I was hoping to hear something else. I hung up from him and began to write a letter:

To Whom It May Concern:

This is to inform you that currently CBI is experiencing political differences in Honduras. CBI's assets have been temporarily restrained from functioning in their full capacity. While we continue to solve this problem we are concerned that this may be material in nature. Additional information is available upon request.

Sincerely,

Adam Rousselle.

The hourglass had just been flipped over and the sand was quickly filling at the bottom.

Chapter 18. A New Direction

We were behind with our creditors, but we weren't completely lost. I traveled back to Germany, Greece, Italy, and Japan in hopes of increasing our cash flow. It was quickly becoming painfully evident that CBI as we knew it was dead.

This was a painful realization and one that I did not want to face, but the writing was no longer on the wall. It was written throughout all the newspapers in Honduras, where Correra and his goons continued to wage their war against us.

Honduran Congresswoman Victoria Contreras had teamed up with her old partner, Judge Galeano, and the vultures were circling. "How could I let this happen on my watch? I had to fix it . But there were simply some things I couldn't fix.

As I sat at the hotel bar in Athens Greece, following one of my meetings, the bartender strode over to me and said that the front desk had been trying to reach me. As I approached the front of the hotel, I was hoping that everything was okay with Catherine. It was Easter, and though I was never particularly religious, I felt guilty about being away from her during the Holy Week. I was relieved when I heard Argentina de Batres on the other end.

But she was crying. Almost inconsolable.

"Adam. You have to call Joe's doctor."

"What's going on?"

She cried louder which only made me more concerned, but she wouldn't tell me any specifics.

"You have to talk to him yourself."

"Okay. But is Dad okay?"

"He is here in Honduras."

"Okay. Please just calm down. I will call Dr. Kahn now."

"Thank you Adam. Thank you. It's so bad. It's so bad."

Argentina de Batres had a real flare for the dramatic, but the tone in her voice worried me. I picked up the receiver and called Dad's doctor in Florida, Dr. Kahn. Of course he didn't answer but his assistant put me on hold, once I told her who I was. Dr. Kahn had been expecting my call. Something was wrong with Dad, obviously, and I couldn't help but think his diabetes or hypertension had gotten worse.

"Mr. Adam."

Dr. Khan and I had never spoken before. Dad was not one to share his medical information and he had long forbidden me to inquire about his medical health no matter what. Well, he was in Honduras, and I was in Greece, so his wishes were irrelevant.

"Mrs. Argentina asked me to talk to you about your father Joe."

Dr. Khan's formality scared me, though I realized that his tone was part of who he was.

"What's going on with him."

"He has stage 4 colon cancer. We will begin an aggressive radiation treatment immediately in hopes of prolonging his quality of life."

I went numb. I'm not sure I heard Dr. Kahn say something about medications and diet, but it was all inaudible garble to me.

When we hung up, I became angry. I became angry because this was something that I could not fix. It pissed me off that the Honduran government, led by Correra was really messing with my Dad at this time while he was battling *cancer*. How could those assholes think they would get away with it.

Dad knew that I knew his diagnosis, but he still tried to downplay it like he did with everything.

"It's nothing. I'm going to take these medicines they've given me and Argentina has set me up at the hospital here in La Ceiba. I should be fine."

But he wasn't fine and I couldn't help but wonder how long he had known. My mind went back to that trip to Florida when he went to see his doctor. Did he find out then? Had he refused treatment at that time. The questions were endless and as I sat in Lamaze Class with Catherine back in Kentucky, I was grateful for the mental relief. The joy I felt about Adam's pending birth was indescribable. Thinking of him and our family was my only escape as I ran endlessly on the hamster wheel of my life; trying to keep us afloat.

But that euphoria was short lived.

Omar Canales, legal representative of COHDEFOR, came forward to prove that the wood we had in the containers was illegal. He started out by saying that the containers were in fact under Judicial Embargo, which was of course untrue unless some Judge I had never heard from, did something that was not recorded anywhere in any legal process. The lying son-of-a-bitch went on to say that the Transportation Permits of the Permit holders that CBI bought from included two from a stolen set [talonario] for which somehow CBI was responsible for!

Honduras had the same laws as in the States; good faith purchase is sufficient. But he wasn't done. This genius then said that the Transportation Permits did not indicate CBI as the buyer and therefore were null and void. This was all a product of Sandoval Correra's refusal to accept that there was a free market and it had no legal validity whatsoever.

Apparently there were witnesses to all of this bullshit who said that COHDEFOR agents were told the transport was to CBI and insisted on putting someone named "Dracosa" on the paperwork. I had no clue who the heck Dracosa was, because it was all made up in Sandoval Correra's dreams.

The only thing Omar Conales got right was that CBI's business was the buying and selling of lumber but then he said we weren't legally authorized to operate. He quoted a non-existent Law and said that "the wood was illegal because it was not a local purchase." *What the fuck was he talking about?*

"Local purchase" was an administratively imposed concept of Sandoval Correra that only groups of *campesinos* could cut trees and they had to sell locally. This notion was diametrically opposed to existing law.

These trumped up "findings" allowed Correra to then go back to Judge Galeano and he charged CBI with "illegally cutting wood from the Honduran National Forest." Undoubtedly, he believed that this would stick no matter what. This was a Sovereign Law of Honduras that could not be contested.

I frantically tried to reach Mitch McConnell but to no avail. I contacted Mike McKee at the U.S. Embassy in Honduras, but he told me there was nothing he could do. He worked in Commercial Affairs and all they could really do was essentially provide moral support. Billy Piper, Mitch McConnell's Chief of Staff phoned back to let me know that they had reviewed all of the

THE MAHOGANY MAFIA   135

information and had made several calls on my behalf, but it "wasn't U.S. policy to get involved in these types of matters where Sovereign law applied." He did offer that Senator McConnell would be willing to write a letter on my behalf and send it to the appropriate people, but that was the extent of what he could do.

We were screwed.

I made the painful decision that we *had* to file for personal and corporate bankruptcy. This was going to change so many things in our lives, but it was the only choice that I could see. Still, I didn't quit. CBI may have folded (due to no fault of our own), but I had to maintain a good life for Catherine and Adam.

In my years of importing mahogany, I always wanted to share its beauty. I shipped two entire flatbeds of kiln-dried mahogany to Pine Valley Golf Course. The deal I made was simple: use it to make our clubhouse the most comfortable and elegant in Kentucky, and I get free Maker's Mark and golf until I die. Hands were shaken, and today you can walk into that clubhouse and see our handiwork. Ed Hawkins, a man of great integrity, once stood up for me in the neighborhood when tongues were wagging. His honorable mention during trying times demonstrated his loyalty and character. I won't forget how much his support mattered.

I decided to launch a new venture called Rousselle Trading Company. I was already working on selling American hardwoods around the world. Now I would just do it under the umbrella of a new company while the bankruptcy proceedings began.

Wood Products, Hogue, Beard, Holz Braun, Nichinan, Moxon, Yao Leun, AWP, Marmiroli, Hibdon Hardwood, Healdsberg Ca, Luthier's Mercantile, (Owned by Theodor Nagle), Olfhausen Billiards, Evangellos Greece, Gillas, Greece, Haute Grips; I called everyone. My life was thrust once again into this whirlwind of phone calls, trips, faxes, letter writing and Lamaze classes.

In between I had to inventory all our personal items for the bankruptcy proceedings. Catherine and I filed for Chapter 7 protection. It was devastating for us both, but the pain in her eyes as we filled out the paperwork broke my heart.

We were not going to be able to pay our creditors and to make matters worse, Stewart Sexton had popped up.

Stewart wrote a letter to Dad explaining some things that he had "heard." He faxed it to him at the LaQuinta. It read:

"I received the following bits and pieces from Caoba de Honduras: The current president of the country owns or is the principal owner in a timber company. 2. Mahogany CBI was selling was never paid for. The government was never paid and thus we (Nordisk) bought it on the Black Market. 3. The lumber will go to auction unless CBI pays the government for the lumber. 4. Joe Rousselle was put in jail temporarily about the matter. 5. Adam Rousselle can not go back to Honduras for fear of arrest, Please regard, Stewart Sexton."

Michael Canahuati. How did he know all this information and why didn't he tell me and why would he tell Stewart? I had sent Stewart the letter letting him know about what was going on with CBI and the fact that I thought the matter would be resolved. The Bills of Lading showed that CBI was legally authorized to ship the lumber and it was going to Nordisk. It was Nordisk's property. When I got the letter, I contacted Stewart to give him the facts and let him know that we could get him his money back.

"I don't want the money. I want the lumber."

"They won't give it to us. It's all bullshit."

"I will look into it."

That was it. That was all that he had to say about it. Nordisk was a major international company with strong ties all over the world. I figured that Stewart would be able to help in all of this and at the least get his lumber, which would close our books with him.

I found out from our attorney that in order to complete the bankruptcy, we had to close all of our credit cards. I had personal money set aside for Catherine and I at least for a little while, but Dad survived on my credit cards. This was how he paid for everything that he needed, including his medications, food and room at the La Quinta.

"What do you mean I can't use it?"

"I mean. We have to stop using it completely. I have to close the account or otherwise it would be fraud."

"I don't have anything else."

I knew this was true and as much as it hurt me to see the look on Catherine's face as we filed our bankruptcy paperwork, the sound of Dad's voice was nearly as troubling. He didn't have anything else. He had given his entire life to CBI and was a major reason for its success. Sure, I did the traveling and sold the lumber, but Dad managed the company and the local relationships that allowed us to thrive. He never asked for much in return, but I always tried to make sure he got his just due.

"What about my medicines?"

"I'll cover those."

"Insurance?"

"I will do my best to make sure you're okay Dad. Trust me on that. Don't you worry."

"Okay Adam."

There was a twinge of sadness in his voice that I had not heard before. As if he finally realized this was truly the end.

But Dad wasn't the only one suffering. Jimmy had gone into hiding for fear of arrests himself. Correra had openly accused him of having incestual relationships with his daughters to try and pressure him out of hiding, but Jimmy didn't bite. First he went to ground (hiding in Olancho) then to La Ceiba. The newspapers with Correra pulling the strings, fried him alive. He had no access to cash and was desperate when he reached out to me.

"Adam can I sell the trucks."

"Yeah Jimmy. Anything you need."

"I need cash. Badly. It's bad times down here."

"Get out of there Jimmy."

"I will."

When we hung up, I thought that would be the last time I would ever hear from Jimmy, but I was wrong. He called me a week later to ask me if he could *take he trucks apart and sell them* because he was having problems selling the trucks and knew he could sell the parts. That's the kind of stand up guy Jimmy was. I didn't give a shit. The trucks were gone as far as I was concerned, but Jimmy, always staying true to his word, wanted to let me know that he had to change part of the plan. I guess that was the former military man in him.

Correra and the Honduran government set a trial for CBI. They assigned Lillian Padilla as our attorney. We lost the trial before it even got started.

Galeano was the judge. Contreras was lurking in the shadows and Correra was always looking from above, ensuring that his masterful plan was executed without a hitch. We had no witnesses and none of us were there.

It was a farce to say the least. I learned that Padilla had been arrested months before for impersonating an attorney, yet they assigned her to represent us. But things got worse. Out of nowhere Stewart Sexton showed up and told the court that "Joe Rousselle had cheated him!

What!

Stewart went on to say that CBI under Joe's direction had knowingly taken money from him knowing that the containers were never going to be delivered. This was a nail in Dad's coffin. I was flabbergasted. I couldn't believe that Stewart would walk into a courtroom and lie about this. It was all his idea to buy more lumber, ship it with a different transportation company, and when we did, we had no idea of any impoundments, and now he had told the entire country of Honduras that we had cheated him. In one fatal swoop, he had ruined the reputation that we had worked endlessly to foster with the people of Honduras.

The fallout was swift and aggressive. Dad was arrested immediately, and his face was plastered all over the newspapers in Honduras with Stewart's quotes and accusations. I received several faxes of pictures of him in handcuffs with an incredulous look on his face of "How could you do this to me?" Correra then had 13 more of our former employees arrested and thrown into prison as well. The message was clear, "We want you Adam Rousselle."

I received a call from someone in Correra's office with a simple message.

"If you return to Honduras, we will set everyone free. Including your father."

"Fuck you."

I slammed the phone down and instead withdrew money from my personal account to pay for each person to get out of jail. It cost me $36,000.

But they wouldn't release my Dad.

Chapter 19. And Then There Were Three

It was crucial for me to get Dad out of jail as soon as possible. I called everyone that I could possibly think of and I wrote another letter to senator McConnell's office pleading for them to intervene and get him released. Billy Piper called me and promised that he would do the best that he could.

Stewart's testimony about feeling that we had duped him had ramifications far beyond financial fallout for us in Honduras. And even though I was wasn't there, I could still feel the sting of his words and those that followed from people I had considered to be some of our closest confidants, beginning with Judy Salazar.

Judy had courted our business throughout our entire existence and we had built a strong relationship with her. But she echoed Stewart's sentiments and told the judge in Honduras that she was worried that we would not pay our debts!

Unbelievable!

Our total debt at the time that we were closed was less than $120,000. That was our *total* debt.

For the amount of money that we had put into Banco Atlantida over the past year and half, I couldn't believe that she had said that. But it went much deeper.

I hadn't spoken to Luis in months. When things started going badly for us, Dad gave him some money and told him to take care of his family. Luis didn't want to leave, but Dad warned him that staying meant irreparable damage financially and socially for Luis. He reluctantly left. And I thought that was the last we would ever hear from him. But Luis loved my father as a brother and he wasn't going to leave him completely.

"That is her brother."

I was shocked to hear Luis's voice on the other end of the phone, but the shit he just unloaded on me threw me for a tailspin. He was referring to Hernan and Judy Salazaar.

Hernan Lleva, our accountant and the man who oversaw our finances was the brother of Judy Salazaar.

Luis said that some of the other workers had known this and everyone figured that I had also. It was unspoken Honduran law that you didn't volunteer information about other people.

"No way."

This information made me immediately playback some of our dealings with Judy. The way that she always knew when we had big pending deals and would call to solicit loans or some other business transaction. The way that Hernan Lleva always seemed to know when Banco Atlantida would be coming around before anyone else in the office had a clue.

How could I have not seen this?

But Luis didn't call to solely talk about Hernan Lleva. He had something else on his mind.

"I know people who can get to him."

"Who?"

"Correra."

"No. We don't want that."

I knew what Luis was talking about and I couldn't have that on my hands. No matter what, I wasn't interested in breaking the law in any sort of way

"How's your daughter?" I changed the subject to try and lighten the mood.

Luis loved talking about his family and when he got excited he would switch from English to Spanish, sometimes mid-sentence.

In the end, I thanked him and he promised me that he would make sure that "no one fucked with Joe."

When we hung up, I hurried to my office in the house. Boxes were everywhere because of the packing we had to do to move. I found what I was looking for: a copy of the newspaper that had reported about our Executives being arrested. I scanned the names and just as I thought; no Hernan Lleva.

That scumbag had been a part of this whole thing all along.

Catherine was very pregnant now. Adam was an active baby and she was often uncomfortable and tired. I felt horrible that in addition to being pregnant and about to deliver our baby, Catherine had to watch as our world collapsed around us, but still she powered through it all.

THE MAHOGANY MAFIA

Things were moving quickly.

My lawyers told me that if we were granted Chapter 7 Bankruptcy, then everything would have to go. Our house, the car; everything. The auditor had been spending hours at a time, poring over our personal and financial documents; combing through everything to try and see if we were in fact hiding something. It was an invasive and demeaning process.

Additionally because our house was going to be repossessed, we had to go through a sheriff sale in Kentucky. This meant that our mortgage lender was going to auction off our house that we had worked so hard to make into our home.

To do this, the appraisers needed to come to the house. All of this required paperwork and appointments on top of everything else that we were dealing with.

Lamaze class. Sell wood. Lamaze class. Sell more wood. Meeting. Appointment. Repeat.

Something had to give. My mind was overcome with thoughts. How could I help Dad? What was going to happen to him? How could we live? What could I do?

Rousselle Trading Company was barely keeping us afloat. I decided that I need to expand my reach and I started contacting companies in Saudi Arabia and Kuwait. This was no easy process, and I had to send each company a fax, one page at a time. This was inefficient and with so many irons in the fire, I lacked the patience to do it this way.

I tore through the fax machine manual, looking for a way around this. If I was going to be a global company working in Kentucky, I needed to be able to get information to potential buyers quickly. I toyed with the fax machine a bit and soon learned how to program it, so that I could send multiple faxes at the same time. I coined this the "merge-fax" and after a few trails and a few errors, I perfected the system.

I would go to the office and send out nearly 100 faxes during the night when I wasn't there. It was ingenious. Our one-man operation worked like I had a team of 10 salespeople, all busting their asses to make money.

For any lumber we shipped, we painted a big blue strip on the edges and wrote "ROUSSELLE" on top of it on every bundle of lumber that we shipped and sold from our warehouse in Kentucky.

Our customers appreciated it and it gave them comfort knowing that the quality of wood they received from CBI would still be sold from Rousselle Trading Company.

One day in August, Catherine and I sat down to work out on our expenses and cost of living. The court date for our bankruptcy was approaching and once it was finalized our financial future was uncertain.

"Why aren't we successful at this level?"

Catherine's question was sincere and revealing.

We realized that we had made a ton of connections and helped a lot of people, but we weren't rich as people might have expected. We had done so much to help so many other people.

I had no real answer to her question and all I could respond with was,

"I don't know, except that we had $10,000,000.00 in inventory that the stole from us. That's where our profits are.

Except for that I truly didn't know the answer. But what I did know was that Rousselle Trading Company was not going to be able to sustain us. I had to find other means to make money.

Months earlier I had floated the idea to Theodore Nagle about working with him and Peter Weiss in sales. He had said he would hire me, but the timing simply hadn't been right. I had started Rousselle Trading Company in the meantime, and we hadn't broached the subject again.

Weise trusted me and believed in me. He brought me on to help with their sales, while allowing me to still work under the Rousselle Trading Company Banner. We created a new partnership, built more on the strength of his belief in me than for a need to have me on board.

Every day was a new day in the art of "making something out of nothing." It was a daily scramble and no matter what, I always felt like I was running in quicksand.

I did get some good news form Billy Piper in Senator McConnell's office. They had managed to get someone from the Honduran Ambassador's office to visit my Dad at Penal La Ceiba. Dad shared an open cell with 50 other prisoners. The conditions, Billy told me (which I already knew) were deplorable, but Dad seemed to be doing well. Billy assured me that someone from the Ambassador's office would check in on him regularly to ensure that he was being treated fairly.

This was a relief to hear, but Dad still wasn't free. I sent some of our savings and paid for some of his medications to be shipped to Honduras so that they could be given to him by whomever visited him from the Ambassador's office. Catherine and I were nearly out of money.

We had a visit with our OB/GYN, Dr. Link on August 11th. Adam was coming soon. Dr. Link advised us that because Catherine was so petite, and Adam was going to be a big baby, we would have a cesarean section birth. We scheduled the procedure for a few days later on August 14th.

I had a meeting scheduled for that morning at the Lexington Hilton and Catherine's Mom, Gerri, came into town to be with us. I took her and Catherine to the hospital to prep for Adam's arrival, then rushed over to my meeting.

I couldn't really understand a word that the guy was saying. We talked about trying to expand the timber business in the states and he mentioned a potential partnership of some sort. I kept looking at my watch, which I hated to do, but he understood.

"Cherish every moment, because they're gone very quickly."

I thanked him and rushed out to get back to the hospital. I had this overwhelming sense that I wouldn't be there when Adam was born, and the doctors would be looking for me. I couldn't let that happen no matter what and I drove like a maniac, until I arrived.

I ran inside to Catherine's pre-op room and sat down beside her. She held out her hand and I wrapped my fingers around hers. She smiled at me.

"We're going to be alright."

I fought back the tears welling up in my eyes. I was afraid.

I made my way to the waiting room. Catherine was already in the operating room. Gerri was there and we sat together talking.

"You're going to be just fine."

"I know"

I was in the labor and delivery room holding Catherine's hand and watching the doctors having trouble with the surgery, It was clear to me something was really wrong when the nurses started to get rattled. They had to cut more than they thought, and Catherine was bleeding badly.

In that moment I couldn't help also being focused on where we would live when our house was sold. How was I going to take care of my family? How could I afford to feed Adam? Diapers? I drove myself crazy trying to answer questions that had no answers and an overwhelming sense of guilt for even thinking about business at the same time Catherine's surgery was going badly.

Adam was amazing. When I held him, I couldn't stop crying. I had never known that sort of joy. He fit perfectly in my arms. Seeing him sleeping quietly reinvigorated me and made all my worries disappear. I had work to do and nothing was ever going to stop me from accomplishing what I needed to do to take care of him and Catherine.

Catherine and Adam soon came home and Gerri was there to provide the best support that she could possibly have given. She took notes for me and helped me get organized. I had to meet with Judge Dickinson with my lawyers and we had to sell the house. I also had to return the BMW that we were leasing.

I dropped it off at the BMW dealership in Lexington and didn't even look back. It was a bump in the road that was only going to make me stronger. I sent out merge faxes all over the world and filled several orders. I even sent Dad more medicines and money. He could buy himself food from the outside or anything else that he needed. That was just how penal life worked in Honduras.

I had a trip coming up to Taiwan, Italy, and some other stops in Europe. I decided that this would be a good trip to take my Mom with me.

She hadn't been out of the country before and I was excited to show her the world. She had no idea that I was going through a bankruptcy and even if she did, she would have told me that everything would be okay.

I arrived for our hearing at the Bankruptcy Court on September 14th, exactly a month after Adam was born. I was confident that our bankruptcy would be approved. My lawyer said the proceedings should take a couple of days at the most, unless someone contested it. From all indications that wasn't going to happen, so I thought we'd be in and out and I would spend the rest of the month rebuilding a new life for my family of three.

My lawyers and I walked into the court room and it was nearly empty. As I approached my seat, I glanced to the left…

… and there was Stewart Sexton.

Critical Intervention Arrives

My face went flush, and I could feel my blood begin to boil. Stewart Sexton had no business at my bankruptcy hearing. I leaned into my lawyer.

"What the hell is he doing here?"
"He's contesting your bankruptcy. As a creditor of yours, he has the right."

"That's bullshit. I don't owe him anything."

That *bastard*. I couldn't' stop cursing under my breath and I didn't even care if the judge heard me. I was angry and frustrated. Dad was in jail in Honduras. Adam had just been born. Catherine was tired. And money was scarce. This bankruptcy had to be approved. Or else, I wasn't sure what would happen to Catherine, Adam or me. All I could do was think of the tough times that my Mom had when my Dad left us.

I couldn't put my family through that sort of struggle.

The Honorable Charles M. Allen, Senior Judge United States District Judge Western District of Kentucky in Louisville presided over my case. He wasted no time getting started. As he read over my claims, he paused to ask was there anyone who disputed my claims.

Stewart Sexton immediately arose.

"On behalf of Nordisk, I do." Stewart spoke clearly without looking at me. Of course he didn't look at me. He was a liar and a coward.

"We believed that Adam Rousselle, Joe Rousselle and CBI knowingly defrauded Nordisk of 14 containers of lumber and we want our money back."

Judge Allen looked at me point blankly. I instantly felt as though he didn't believe me. It didn't matter if I was a decorated war hero or a distinguished officer. Or even a tax-paying local businessman who employed native Kentuckians. Stewart sounded serious and that counted for something.

"Is this true Mr. Rousselle?"

"Hell no. It's not."

"Then what grounds is Mr. Sexton making this claim."

"I don't know. Ask him."

For the next few days, Stewart Sexton depicted me as a person who knowingly defrauded Nordisk and my other creditors. He rationalized to the Judge that because of the swift nature in which I filed bankruptcy after taking draws from my credit lines, I embezzled the money and not lived up to the agreement that I had with Nordisk.

Because of the speed in which this occurred, it appeared to creditors that I should have known that I was about to go out of business when I had taken recent draws from my credit line.

Nordisk was suing me for the price it had paid for the lumber. I had no means of paying it back, since the lumber had been confiscated and my business in Honduras was shut down.

Stewart Sexton knew this.

He didn't mention though that I told him, we would pay him back months ago and he said he wanted the lumber instead. Piece of shit.

My life was hell. I kept wondering how all of this could happen. I was the good guy. I was trying to help people and give them a better life in a country that couldn't afford to help its own people. And all I had to show for it now was my Dad being in jail and my world slowly crumbling around me.

My lawyers disputed Sexton's claims, but it didn't seem to work. The judge took meticulous notes and by the looks of things the bankruptcy wasn't going to be approved. When we walked in on the day for him to render his decision, I had a sense of gloom hanging over me all day.

The only joy I could find was seeing Adam and Catherine.

I tried to imagine myself back home with them, in a different time and place, where this shit wasn't happening.

"Excuse me your honor. I'd like to speak."

"Damn," I thought. Not another one. My lawyers had warned me that other creditors may come forward. I watched as the woman approached the Judge.

"My name is Emily Claire Leonard. And I believe that I can shed some light on this situation on behalf of Mr. Rousselle and CBI Lumber."

This got my attention. I felt as though I had heard the name before, and she looked vaguely familiar. She was perhaps in her 50's, nondescript, but exuded an air of confidence and intellect that I instantly knew could only mean one thing…

THE MAHOGANY MAFIA 147

"What is it that you would like to share Ms. Leonard?"

Judge Allen seemed disinterested and cynical about whatever it is that she had to say, but she was unfazed. She strode to the front and stood before him.

"I was the Assistant Station Chief of the Central Intelligence Agency in Honduras I am here on behalf of the United States Federal Government."

... I knew it. There was just an air about Intelligence Officers that separated them from everyone else. It didn't matter if it was a man or a woman. When someone from Intelligence entered a room, other Intelligence officers like myself instantly knew it. It was as if we had some sort of unspoken link that years of quiet observation and diligent note taking created.

Judge Allen was shocked. His demeanor instantly shifted. I smiled, though I had no clue what she was about to say, but I knew whatever it was it was going to help me. I glanced over at Stewart Sexton, and he shifted uncomfortably in his seat. I guessed that he knew more than I did about what Emily Leonard had to say.

"This should be good." Judge Allen sat back in his chair. Ready for the details.

I studied her for a moment, as she pushed her glasses back up on her nose. She reached into her briefcase and retrieved a mountain of documents. And then she began to speak...

"I am a U.S. citizen currently residing in Tegucigalpa, Honduras. I am a retired USAID Senior Foreign Service Officer, currently in my third of the five years of law school the State provides here. I had been assisting Joseph (Joe) Rousselle since July in trying to resolve the completely irregular criminal processes against him in Honduras. In the process of analyzing the criminal cases I have found documents which clearly indicate that neither Joe or Adam Rousselle could have realized that Honduran customs would want to inspect 11 containers destined for Puerto Cortes on January' 26, I also know that once notified of the hold for inspection on January 30 by Maersk that Customs was holding the containers, CBI had no reason to believe the inspection would not be carried out immediately and knowing that the containers contained no Guayacan, nor were their contents under-declared, had no reason to believe customs wouldn't immediately permit the shipment of the wood..."

I glanced over at Stewart Sexton. He wouldn't dare look my way. My lawyer sat back, not completely sure of where all of this was going. I didn't know either, but I liked the sound of it.

Emily continued...

"...Furthermore, I know that that even the Honduran institutions involved were very confused by the situation and unable to effect the inspection until March 2. I also know that a COHDEFOR employee falsified an official document to cover up all the illegal impoundment of the wood..."

I almost jumped out of my damned seat! *"What the hell was she talking about."* I was just as stunned as Judge Allen and Stewart, who was now no longer the confident looking liar he had once been.

"...This evidence was not provided at the time of U.S. trial by the Rousselle's Honduran attorney, Liliana Padilla, because she was not capable of analyzing the documents, having never been a lawyer or a law student. She has been in jail awaiting trial for impersonating a lawyer and fraud in prejudice of Mr. and Mrs. Joe Rousselle in the criminal cases in la Ceiba and Olanchito..."

Emily then proceeded to provide her background. Honduras had been her last post. She had retired in November of 1994, after serving 24 years and reaching the age of 50 in her Intelligence Service. She decided to attend law school and stay in Honduras, because she wanted to continue to fight Judicial corruption, which she seen run rampant in Honduras.

"...In the five years I served in Honduras, I managed a portfolio of projects totaling $200 million and a staff of 35 people plus contractors for each project. One of these projects was for the improvement of the Administration of Justice. Because of personnel difficulties, from 1990 to 1995 I had to personally manage this project, something which I enjoyed, and to which was able to dedicate a lot of time because the rest of my staff was very competent. Because of my close work with the Honduran Supreme Court, which is not just legally but administratively at the pinnacle of the judicial pyramid, and my role in creating a Justice Department, the Embassy instructed me to investigate all U.S. Citizen criminal cases in which impropriety of the Judges was alleged..."

The courtroom was deadly silent. No one seemed to breathe. Her background was impressive, and I knew she was setting us up to drop the hammer on this whole thing. I thought to myself, *"How did my dad know this woman?"*

But I did know how my Dad knew her because she was an American woman living in Honduras. Gringo Joe knew every American woman in Honduras.

Emily knew that she was in control.

"...Thus I spent five years analyzing Honduran criminal cases so as to recommend to the Embassy the validity of the complaints and possible actions which would help in the cases which had merit. Many times, I simply spoke with the Magistrates directly during our regular project administration sessions and they resolved most of the questionable situations. I explain this so you will understand I have a deep and thorough understanding of the formalities of the criminal process and the standard forms of corruption in the processes. Because of my efforts in behalf of Honduras I was awarded honors by the equivalent of the State Attorney's office , the Supreme Court, the Honduran Bar Association, and The Office of the Inspector General of the Courts ..."

She turned to face my lawyers and I.

"...It is important to understand that Honduras, while technically a country of Law, is in reality not. Criminal suits against business competitors to "sink" them was such a problem that in 1991 the Supreme Court issued an administrative instruction, *Auto Acordado #5*, that in civil matters criminal suits can only be brought after a civil suit has occurred. The Judges routinely ignore or misunderstand this instruction. CBI created a problem for its competitors in that it was closer to the source of supply of hardwood than the other major buyers in San Pedro Sula and this resulted in reduced transportation costs for the sellers. The supply of hardwood, at that time, was irregular and undependable , exacerbating the problem in San Pedro Sula..."

Now it was beginning to come together. I thought about everything that had happened in Honduras and how quickly things seemed to change. The level of corruption and collusion against us reached far deeper than we initially understood. Correas was in fact trying to force us out of business the whole time to make room for Canahuati.

"...Honduras is also a country in which ties of family, politics and friendships are very much more sacred than the Law. There is also a deep hatred for the "Centrist", i.e. America, countries by the primarily ruling Leftist governments. Joe and Adam Rousselle's only crime was that they were Americans, making money from a Honduran resource. In the minds of the Honduran government, they had to be stopped..."

My mind instantly went to my Dad. I always knew he was innocent but to hear these words made it far more painful.

"...So you combine the interests of the hardwood industries in San Pedro Sula (in the Northwest), particularly a company of Mike Canahuati which made a major investment in kilns toward the end of 1994, and the paranoia and hatred of the Director General of COHDEFOR, and the Judge and Assistant D.A. in La Ceiba toward Americans, you have the motives that caused all of CBI's problems; these problems are a result of economic and political interests, not of law..."

What Emily verbalized was something we had known. Even when I was there in the military, many Hondurans simply didn't like Americans, because of the propaganda and bullshit that they had been fed for most of their lives. I wanted to prove them wrong. Dad wanted to prove them wrong. This is why we overpaid our workers and brought them gifts from America on our visits. We wanted to show them that we could all benefit from this business together.

In January of 1994, the Administration of Liberal President Carlos Roberta Reina replaced the open market orientation of the prior administration and named Rigoberto Sandoval Correra Director General of COHDEFOR. Correra was a known Leftist, with strong anti-American ideologies, and the creation and application of administrative regulations completely in conflict with the Law. He had already cost the country $1 million dollars in a lawsuit by a Mexican company. The guy was a complete asshole.

Emily continued to reveal that in early 1994, after CBI had been in business for quite some time, Correra launched a harassment Campaign against us. The memories came flooding back to me. We had been called to Tegucigalpa by a COHDEFOR adviser and asked to bring the equivalent of $5,000 to smooth over any future problems. We complied. We were used to paying "fees," so we didn't think much of it.

"...In early July CBI sought to get a management plan approved by the Regional Director of COHDEFOR so that CBI could cut wood and thus reduce its dependence on the erratic supply situation which in turn would make the plant more efficient. The Director, Jorge Alberto Flores Abud asked them for an "administrative fee" of approximately $30,000. CBI refused and a week later was formally charged in the local court in La Ceiba of illegal trafficking in wood. This was only two weeks after the same Flores Abud had said they were fully authorized to buy from licensed sellers..."

I could see Judge Allen's eyes widen as he listened to Emily's testimony. She was knocking it out of the park and she had the documents to prove her point. Then she dropped the bomb.

"...From this date the La Ceiba criminal process investigatory stage proceeded to dribble forward and the Judge didn't actually move to the point of ordering

THE MAHOGANY MAFIA   151

the accused; Joseph Rousselle, Adam Rousselle, and Jimmy Malone, to testify until March 2, 1995. Two months after Stuart Sexton's lumber had been illegally detained and well after the payments made by Mr. Sexton had been cashed..."

That was all that Judge Allen needed to hear. I saw him jot down notes. I was fuming inside.

My eyes shot to Stewart Sexton. He couldn't avoid me any longer. We locked gazes for just a brief moment. I was waiting for him to stand up and say that Nordisk would withdraw its lawsuit against me. I was waiting for him to admit their part in this whole thing, but it didn't happen. He looked down at his watch as if he was receiving instructions from it on his next move.

From July of 1994 to March of 1995, we received all kinds of accusations. But no one stopped our business. None of our wood was impounded. Emily produced a forged document that in fact had been backdated to January 30, 1995 that said that our lumber had been impounded.

It was all one big lie.

What I learned that day was that this all began in the city of Olanchito with an accusation by the local assistant D.A. for the environment in November 17, 1994. The Judge there worked faster and somewhat more accurately then in La Ceiba. In January He had Dad and Jimmy arrested-to-testify so they could declare their case against us on January 26th. This was the same day that the 11 containers belonging to Stewart Sexton traveled to Puerto Cortes.

They wanted to steal the wood from right under our noses!

The Judge let them out on personal bonds of $80 and fines of $100. The shit sucked but we had no reason to believe something bigger was going on. No one said anything. Getting arrested in Honduras had become par for the course. The reality is CBI's Free Zone status made COHDEFOR hesitant to act even though they had almost incompetent legal representation during this period.

We knew Correra was pissed that he hadn't shut us down.

Emily had one final blow to land before she finished.

"...Two days before Christmas the event occurred which triggered the illegal detainment of the containers. This event could not have been known to anyone in CBI because it was not made public. It was documented in the case file in Olanchito, on either the 28th or 29th of March 1995..."

I thought back to that Christmas. When Stewart Sexton, Canahuati and Steve Sexton had gone ghost. I thought of seeing them together weeks later. The Sextons were behind this whole thing!

"According to the document, a letter from Dr. Carlos Medina, Minister of the Environment, sent to Sandoval Correra, and dated the 23rd of December, 1994, Dr. Medina had received a phone call from Doctor Jose Herrero, General Director of the business enterprise El Marranito in La Ceiba. Dr. Herreo informed Dr. Medina CBI was shipping approximately 11 containers of wood per week which carried 15,000 to 18,000 board feet of wood but were being declared as containing only 11,000 board feet. I investigated and found that this information came to Doctor Medinas attention in a phone call from Jose (Pepe) Marinakys, owner of Agencia Marinakys, a wood products trader, in San Pedro Sula. When contacted by a mutual friend of Joe Rousselle, Mr. Marinakys admitted that he had no personal knowledge of this of the undervaluing; that he had heard about it in a bar. In spite of the fragility of Mr. Herrera's information, Sandoval Correra seems to have been more than ready to believe it with no substantiation."

I slumped slightly in my chair. Not because of defeat, but because I knew I had won a case that should've never happened. I still should've been in Honduras doing business as usual and living in our house in Elizabethtown. Dad should have been free. Jimmy should've been laughing. Everything should've been the same.

I closed my eyes as Emily concluded her testimony.

"On January 26, the same day that Joe Rousselle and Jimmy Malone spent testifying in Olanchito, and 15 days after their arrest-to-testify warrant was issued in La Ceiba at the request of the Judge in Olanchito; it should have been immediately executed but wasn't, interestingly enough, Customs detained the containers. The internal COHDEFOR memo that this information comes from is enlightening in that it shows COHDEFOR, Customs, the State Attorney's Office, and the Port Authority falling over their own feet. I quote it in its entirety to show that not only could Joe and Adam Rousselle not know what was going on, the Honduran institutions didn't know either until closure of an investigation was reached in March when with both Rousselles out of the country, COHDEFOR dummied up a false confiscation..."

Emily stood facing Judge Allen.

"That's all documented here?"

"Yes. Your Honor. It's all here."

"Where is the lumber now that was taken?"

"My guess is it has been sold to Caoba de Honduras"

Our bankruptcy was awarded.

Chapter 20. One Last Phone Call

"Michael Canahuati and John Sexton are business partners. Hernan Leva was feeding them information. His sister is Judy Salazaar by the way."

The words stung me to my core, as I sat across from Emily Leonard at the Last Chance Café in Louisville. I had given Hernan Leva several raises. He knew everything about our company and Judy was our banker. The same banker who was demanding we pay back a $100,000 loan after we had deposited millions of dollars into her bank. I had my suspicions about Stewart Sexton, but I wasn't sure about John.

John oversaw buying furniture parts from Caoba de Honduras. However, Caoba de Honduras never had enough lumber and even if they did, it was not kiln dried and ready for manufacturing. John knew Stewart was buying CBI's lumber, shipping it to Manning South Carolina to be kiln dried and then shipped it back to Honduras to Caoba de Honduras. This was an inefficient, but necessary operational process. John had better ideas, what if he could increase supply and kiln dry his lumber in Caoba de Honduras' facilities? He could save a lot of money and increase output at the same time. His company's motives were clear.

If John could accomplish this, Caoba de Honduras would also benefit. With new Kilns to improve lumber quality, Caoba de Honduras could then export more fully manufactured goods. It made perfect sense and was the logical thing to do.

How to accomplish this transition from a "CBI lumber-Nordisk SC Kiln Dry- Caoba De Honduras-Hickory Chair's furniture plant" to "Caoba de Honduras- Hickory Chair's furniture plant" required some help.

They knew that they would not get CBI to willingly go along with closing CBI's lumber operations. So the next opportunities were to have the Honduran Government help close our sawmill for them.

"Correra was determined to sink CBI at all costs. Once he set his sights on you, you didn't stand a chance."

"What can I do now?" I wanted to sue the shit out of Stewart, John, Correra, Canahuati and anyone else I could think of to get my lumber back.

"Present your case in Federal Court."

I wanted to ask Emily more about her relationship with my Dad, because I could tell every time she mentioned his name, her eyes would light up in a way that told me he had stolen her heart. I decided against it though so as to save both of us from the likely awkwardness that would follow. Some things are just better left unsaid.

Walking into Federal Court with Emily's testimony in hand and her presence made easy work for the court. The Honduran government was found guilty of unlawfully confiscating the assets of an American Company and they owed me $10 million. This sounded great on paper, but there was no way I was going to get that money. I couldn't go back to the country for fear of being arrested and possibly killed, so my case was slightly more than a moral victory, though I figured if I could find the right International Law Firm, I could go after them in the future.

I now had to focus my attention on finding a new home for my family and getting my Dad back home. I made a final plea to Billy Piper in Mitch McConnell's office.

"...We are going to go and get him."

I couldn't believe it. Mitch McConnell had agreed to help me! He authorized the use of a private plane to fly down to Honduras and bring my Dad back. There had been some political maneuvering between the U.S. Ambassador's Office and the Honduran government. My guess was Sandoval Correra had not been privy to these conversations, as I'm sure he would have done everything possible to thwart the efforts.

He would be home in two days.

I panicked a bit, because now I not only had to find a place for my family, I also had to make sure that my Dad was okay. But that was alright, at least I knew he would be back in the States and able to get his treatments and medications. I kept myself busy making calls trying to unload the last bit of wood we had in the Kentucky warehouse. It had to shut down in a couple of weeks, and everything had to go. I wanted to make sure that every employee there had been paid their salaries for all of the time that they worked and of course have something for Catherine and I.

Two days later, I waited impatiently to hear from my Dad. He was to call me from the airplane as he was leaving Honduras, so that we both be rid of Correas and his henchmen's reach.

I jumped when my phone rang.

"Gringo Joe!" I excitedly called my Dad's name, but there was silence. In the background I could hear men speaking in Spanish. Finally, my Dad spoke up.

"Adam, how are you?"
"Great. Where are you?"

"I'm not coming Adam."

"What do you mean, you're not coming?"

"I'm not leaving Honduras."

I wanted to curse my Dad out. Did he realize what had transpired to get him back to this country. This shit was not a game.

"Get on the plane." I tried to sound demanding, but nobody made Gringo Joe do anything.

My Dad began to speak in a light tone.

"They made me go through customs and they wanted me to sign over all our claims or they would not let me go. If I leave this country, you will not have a claim to anything. I have to stay here, so that you can keep fighting to get your shit back."

And then the phone went dead.

I was lost. Had he just been killed? Was he being held hostage? I got a call from Billy Piper and he confirmed that the plane had arrived as planned, but Joe refused to leave. He chose to stay in prison. I thanked Billy for his efforts and passed along my gratitude to Senator McConnell.

He chose to give up his freedom for me.

I had no words for anyone. I was angry at my Dad and angry at myself for ever being mad at him. He was a handful at times, but he had helped me build something out of nothing. CBI would not have existed without Joe Rousselle, and he was now giving his life to ensure that its legacy continued.

What could I say?

I had sent my resume out to several companies, and I finally landed a job at a company in Nashville, Tennessee. Catherine, Adam and I said our final goodbyes to Kentucky, and we drove to our new one bedroom apartment. I thought about many of the friends that we had back in Kentucky.

THE MAHOGANY MAFIA   157

When we were going through our bankruptcy it was almost as if we were a pariah to some people. They stopped speaking to us, even though they had spent many holidays and evenings at hour home in the past.

That bankruptcy was a blemish on our credibility to some people. They believed that it meant that we were stealing or had done something wrong. I stopped trying to explain what happened to people and just let them think what they wanted. I just kept "smiling and waving."

But still, I was determined to regain my name and dignity.

The company I was working for was a mess. It was being run into the ground by a guy that had no clue what he was doing. To make matters worse, I was commuting an hour and half *each way* every day just to get there. I had to find something else. I called up my old pal Peter Wiese and he hired me to run wood purchasing for Luthiers Mercantile in Healdsberg, CA with a promise for me to work from Tennessee . The company was a famous exotic hardwoods supplier which was great for guitars and specialized parts for fine instruments. This was perfect for Nashville.

But Peter started getting pressure for me to move to the company's headquarters in Germany, and eventually I was hired away by General Woods and Veneers from Toronto, Canada. Only problem was the job was in Breezewood, Pennsylvania, a speck on the map right next to the Pennsylvania turnpike.

Things were looking up and we rented a small house in Altoona. I had to drive an hour and half again to and from work, but this time I didn't mind. I'm a native New Yorker. Being in Pennsylvania sort of reminded me of home. I traveled all over the world, but it was a strain on Catherine with Adam. But I was good at my job and opportunities were coming quickly.

Wood Products called and offered me a deal I couldn't refuse. They wanted me to take over exports and they said they would pay for me to go to Wharton. I told my story about starting CBI and Wharton accepted me at the interview without the application.

I moved Catherine and Adam to Willow Grove, Pennsylvania, rented a house and spent 4 days per week at the lumber mill in western Maryland off Deep Creek Lake.

One evening as I was having dinner and we were playing with Adam, there was a knock at our door. Catherine and I looked at each other strangely. Neither one of us was expecting anyone.

I opened the door and there stood Jimmy Malone. I was shocked to see him, but I instantly thought "What is Jimmy doing here."

"Adam." Jimmy laughed in his big hearty laugh and I let him inside. I had to. Jimmy was like family.

Catherine always loved Jimmy; she had spent quite a bit of time with him down in Honduras. He picked up Adam and laughed again.

"Good thing he looks like his Mama."

I hadn't seen Jimmy in months, which is exactly why I was wondering what he was doing here and how did he find us.

Jimmy ended up spending four days with us.

His sister worked for the FBI and she had helped him find us. He had been living in the states and in different countries in the Caribbean. It was good to have him around and reminiscence over tequila and beers about our days in Honduras.

But I knew Jimmy though.

Sure he loved us and all of that, but he hadn't tracked us down to come and kiss Adam and tell Honduran war stories.

"We don't' have anything Jimmy." I looked him square in the eyes. We both knew what I was talking about.

"This is a nice house. Life looks good."

I got up and found the lease to the house. Showed it to him.

"Rental."

Jimmy looked the lease over and quickly handed it back to me.

"Things had been hard. But I'm making it." Jimmy let out a big laugh.

By the time he left, I knew that I would never see Jimmy again. For his own peace of mind, he needed to come and see me, just to make sure I hadn't hidden anything from him. I had made sure he and all of the CBI employees had been paid well. Hell that was why Catherine and I didn't have any money.

But I was fine with that.

When it came time to go to Wharton, Reg, the owner of Wood Products, reneged on the deal and said Wharton was too expensive and they could not afford to lose me. He knew that I would eventually branch out and do my own thing with the Wharton name behind me.

I had already decided that I was going to utilize my expertise and branch out on my own. I figured I had enough experience to start a lumber consulting firm. Besides, I was an entrepreneur at heart. I preferred to be my own boss on my own terms.

No one had the knowledge or the contacts that I had. I could pair buyers and sellers together all over the globe and people trusted me. I started to earn a better living for Catherine and I, but we stayed in our rented home in California. Dad called me every so often from prison, but each time he sounded worse and worse. I was worried about him, and it pained me that there was nothing I could do to help him.

I had to travel to Japan to meet with several customers, and I considered taking Adam and Catherine with me. I found that when I was away from them, I didn't feel complete. The travel was wearing on me and he was growing up so quickly. We were planning on having another child soon and I vowed that things would be different this time. I would do my best to try not to travel so often.

Ultimately, Catherine and I decided that taking our 2-year-old to Japan was not a good idea and I went alone. One day as I was having lunch at my favorite sushi restaurant in Hamakita City, Japan, my waiter approached me.

"Mr. Rousselle, you have a phone call."

I was surprised. My hotel knew that I loved this place, but I wasn't sure why they were calling me. I finished off my cup of sake and headed to the phone just outside of the kitchen. It was one of those black rotary phones and it smelled like fish

"Hello."

"Adam."

It was my Dad. His connection was weak, so I strained to hear. But his voice was strong.

"Dad. How are you? What's going on?"

"I'm going to die Adam." He was solemn and direct.

"Stop saying that."

"It's true. They told me that I am going to die in the next four hours or so. I probably won't make it through the night. I have these black spots all over my body. The cancer has spread to all my organs. I don't think I can come back from this one Son."

I leaned against the sushi bar. Tears began to flow down my cheeks. I couldn't understand how he could talk so cogently, so matter-of-factly, seemingly without pain or struggle.

There was no whisper or scent of death. It was as if he was reporting on the day's activities of the sawmill like he used to do before.

There was so much that I wanted to say, but the words wouldn't come out. Only the tears kept flowing.

"I want you to know that I am very proud of you Son. Please make sure you get your assets back from those motherfuckers."

"I will."

We both paused for a moment.

"Okay, I'm going to go now.."

"Dad... I'm proud of you too. Thank you for everything. I love you."

"I love you."

We hung up. My head throbbed and I got the sudden sensation that my stomach was empty. I made my way back to my table and sat down for a moment. Everyone in that little sushi bar knew what had happened. No one said a word to me, but their eyes showed their condolences.

My Dad, Joe Rousselle died four hours later as expected. He was buried in in the La Ceiba cemetery in Honduras, where he resides still.

We were daring. We had the balls to go to a country where many of the people hated us, simply because of where we were born. We believed in treating those same people fairly and eventually many of them became our biggest supporters. I've often asked myself the question, "What if?" What if that shipment had never been confiscated? What if there was no Sandoval Correra? What if I had invited Michael Canahuati to be a business partner instead of a competitor? I could ask those sorts of questions for days and still come back to the same conclusion.

THE MAHOGANY MAFIA 161

We arrived in the perfect storm. And no matter what happened or changed, The Mahogany Mafia was going to want its cut. After all, that's what the Mafia does right?

We arrived in the perfect storm. And no matter what happened or changed, The Mahogany Mafia was going to want its cut. After all, that's what the Mafia does, right?

The jungle taught me many lessons—about power, greed, and survival. But as I stood on the edge of the mahogany trade, watching fortunes shift like Rio Bonito's current, I realized that this fight was just the skirmish of a larger battle. The same corruption that plagued the jungles of Honduras stretched its tendrils across borders, infiltrating industries I had yet to study.

The next frontier wouldn't be fought with chainsaws and bribes. It would be waged from the skies, where satellites could see what no human eye could. I wasn't done fighting. The timber thieves would soon learn: no matter how far they ran or how deep they hid, there was no escaping the truth.

And so, my journey continues in: Counting Crowns.

A Glimpse Ahead

Alacrity And Dispatch: The Chronicles Of A Citizen-Soldier's Selfless Service

Is a groundbreaking five-book non-fiction series that unearths the extraordinary journey of a man whose relentless pursuit of justice and innovation reshaped industries and challenged corruption. Documented with meticulous precision, the series ties together seemingly disparate events—from counting timber in the jungle to exposing systemic corruption in America's power grid—into a cohesive story of courage, ingenuity, and resilience. Every chapter is rooted in firsthand accounts and the author's own technological breakthroughs, illustrating how a singular focus on accountability can ignite transformative change. With no names hidden and no detail spared, the books reveal not only the author's remarkable achievements but also the deeper, interconnected forces shaping our modern world.

Coming Next: Counting Crowns: Catching Criminals From Space

Revenge, innovation, and justice from above. When counting timber turns into a national emergency, the author's collaboration with NASA results in technology that revolutionizes vegetation management and facility ratings for transmission utilities. This breakthrough not only combats corruption in the timber industry but also reveals the vulnerabilities in America's power grid, tying environmental mismanagement to critical infrastructure failures.

www.ingramcontent.com/pod-product-compliance
Lightning Source LLC
Chambersburg PA
CBHW052037030426
42337CB00027B/5044